EFF THIS! MEDITATION

MEDITATION

108 TIPS, TRICKS & IDEAS FOR WHEN YOU'RE FEELING ANXIOUS, STRESSED OUT, OR OVERWHELMED

Liza Kindred

Text © 2019 by Liza Kindred

First published in 2019 by Rock Point,
an imprint of The Quarto Group,
142 West 36th Street, 4th Floor, New York, NY 10018, USA
T (212) 779-4972 F (212) 779-6058 www.QuartoKnows.com

Rock Point titles are also available at discount for retail, wholesale, promotional and bulk purchase. For details, contact the Special Sales Manager by email at specialsales@quarto.com or by mail at The Quarto Group, Attn: Special Sales Manager, 100 Cummings Center Suite, 265D, Beverly, MA 01915, USA.

ISBN: 978-1-63106-636-8

Library of Congress Cataloging-in-Publication Data available

Publisher: Rage Kindelsperger
Creative Director: Laura Drew
Managing Editor: Cara Donaldson
Project Editor: Keyla Pizarro-Hernández
Cover and Interior Design: Amy Sly

2 4 6 8 10 9 7 5 3 1

Printed in China

This book provides general information on forming positive habits. However, it should be relied upon as recommending or promoting any specific diagnosis or method of treatment for a particular condition, and it is not intended as a substitute for medical advice or for direct diagnosis and treatment of a medical condition by a qualified physician. Readers who have questions about a particular condition, possible treatments fro that condition, or possible reactions from the condition or its treatment should consult a physician or other qualified healthcare professional. The author and publisher are in no way responsible for any actions or behaviors undertaken by the reader of this book.

TABLE
of
CONTENTS

To my daughter, Veronika, in all of her transitions.

To Alyssa Loren, in her transition.

And to you:
May you be happy, healthy, and well.
May you feel loved.
May you find peace.

HOW TO USE THIS BOOK

First and foremost:

The practices in this book are designed to help you feel good. If something doesn't feel good to you, drop it without judgement and try something else.

If something doesn't jive, it doesn't mean that the book doesn't work, that you did it wrong, or that there is something wrong with you. It means that one technique didn't work for you, so you can move along. Totally cool.

That being said, there are a number of ways you can dive into this book. Do what works for you.

Options for how to use this book:

- Read it all the way through.
- Flip through and mark what seems interesting.
- Try all of the techniques, one by one.
- Grab the book in a panic and thumb through until something sticks out.
- Open the book to a random page and do that thing.
- However the eff you want to do it; it's your book now!

 Any page with this cool icon means there is more bonus material online. All book extras can be found at **effthismeditation.com/bookextras**.

INTRODUCTION

I wrote this book for you. I wrote it because something has happened out there in the world where even when we are trying to find wellness, we are being told we need to constantly fix or heal or improve ourselves—as if something inside of us is inherently broken; as if the problems live inside of us, and not out there in a world that has nearly lost its collective mind.

Jiddu Krishnamurti, the twentieth-century Indian mystic, philosopher, and poet once said,

"It is no measure of health to be well adjusted to a profoundly sick society."

He's so right on. If you feel crazy, or anxious, or sad, or depressed, or overwhelmed, that makes sense. And it is not because you are broken or can't cope—it's because the world is in a state right now.

But that state is not us. And just because we are stressed to the max and freaked the eff out doesn't mean that we have to live like that. Here in this book are 108 practices—simple, private, often free—that you can do in order to find that place of beauty, calm, and equanimity that already exists inside of you. We're not fixing, and we're not creating something new. We're just taking the time to get in touch with the parts of us that already exist simultaneously with the anxiety and sadness and stress. We're letting the parts of us that are loving and calm and compassionate and kind come to the surface sometimes, too.

This book will not try to fix you, because you are not broken, but it will give you many tools and practices to feel more grounded, to disconnect from technology and reconnect to your own heart and body, and to live your life with a little more intention.

You don't have to listen to the voices telling you to hustle harder, work smarter, recover faster, deal better, or whatever other admonishment is swirling around (whether those voices are coming from other people or from inside your own head). And hey, listen: the stressors will *always* be there. The only way to have time to do these practices is to *take* the time. You deserve it.

Georgia ♡

Eff This! Meditation might seem like an unlikely name, but I created this style of meditation two years ago in an effort to be as authentic as possible; after a decade of practicing meditation and studying Buddhism with highly respected teachers, I found that I still, well, get fed up sometimes! We frequently see a version of meditation that is whitewashed (it started in the Eastern world, after all) and is all visions of bliss and enlightenment and very flexible people with perfect skin. That just doesn't jive with my personal experience.

As I teach it, meditation and true self-care are gritty, raw, and real. My offering to the world is a style of meditation that is deeply rooted in the foundational teachings of Buddhism, but presented through the language and experiences of most of our everyday lives. Think of this as meditation with a strong grasp but a light touch.

In a meditation or self-care practice, there are moments of pure peace–that's what we're going for! But mixed into that there are messy emotions and second-guessing and pets climbing on you. This is all fine, because it's real life. When we add the rough edges of the path toward enlightenment to the chaos of the world we're living in, it's enough to make anyone want to scream, "Eff this!"

ME ✦ LOVE

We're often holed up inside, hunched over our devices, over-scheduled and undernourished. We hold our breath while we send emails and we zone out while we scroll through social media. We exercise because we feel bad about our bodies, or we don't work out and feel bad for that. What we try to get done in a day is literally impossible, yet somehow we beat ourselves up for not getting through it all. If you can relate to any of this, let me assure you: these are not personal character flaws, or things for you to beat into submission. This is the fabric of modern life! Technology is designed to be addictive, our modern food system has scientists in labs trying to make junk food more addictive, and entire industries are centered around making us feel too fat or short or poor. Darling, it's not you!

And because we are all living in that craziness every day, you will find some key threads woven through these exercises. These are specific paths toward true wellness that work because they directly address what's driving us all mad.

These are:

☐ Meditation
☐ Nature
☐ Movement
☐ Breathing

☐ Balancing creation with consumption
☐ Creating space
☐ More mindful use of technology

Try some of each category. It will pay off!

I've learned about these things over the course of my life, but especially during the last decade, during which I've been learning to live with a mysterious, life-changing, chronic illness—and as I moved from being a meditator to also being a meditation teacher, and from teaching people how to build disruptive technology to teaching them how to build tech that stops disrupting people's lives.

Some of these things I knew, and then forgot about and discovered again. Some I employ all the time, like hardworking old friends. Some of them came from my personal army of healers. Some of them came from you, the people who have supported my work for many years. Wherever they came from, my hope and intention is that within this book you find things to help you lead a more peaceful life.

By doing the exercises in this book—by taking care of ourselves—we are actually doing the work to make the world a better place. If you can't take care of yourself for you, do it for the rest of us. We deserve the best of you.

This, right here, is your permission to be gentle with yourself, no matter what. This is your permission to make taking care of your physical, mental, emotional, and spiritual health a top priority.

No one deserves happiness more than you.

May this book, and these practices, uncover more peace, joy, and happiness in your life.

Love, Liza

One-Minute Practices

Sometimes we literally only have a minute. That's okay! Just sixty seconds, when spent with intention, can ground us, bring us back into connection with our body, reset our point of view, or put us back in touch with what matters most.

Many of these practices can be done privately, even when we're with other people. Try as many of these as you can, and keep the ones that help you the most in your proverbial back pocket. Whether you're standing in line, sitting in a stressful meeting, or spinning out with anxious thoughts, these practices offer a quick reset when you need it most.

There will always be times when you "need a minute," and this section offers a variety of ways in which you can take that quick time out.

Inbreath < outbreath

This is as close as it gets to a magic trick.

If you remember just one thing from this book, let it be this: our breath is the only system in our bodies that we can either control or not, and we can take over direct control of our nervous system by making conscious choices about how we breathe.

When we choose to make our outbreath even slightly longer than our inbreath, we are sending a direct message of relaxation to our brain.

Think of when we are panicking: we sip or gasp in lots of air, which prepares us for fight-or-flight mode. Focusing on a longer exhale tells our autonomous nervous system that it can stand down instead. It also clears out the lungs and prepares us to receive more fresh oxygen.

You can do this anytime, anywhere. Just take a few (preferably deep) breaths, where you count your inbreath and give your outbreath a count of a couple more.

That's it. You just lowered your own heart rate a bit.

See-hear-feel
A.K.A. 3-3-3

This is a quick trick to connect you to the present moment. Take a deep breath and just notice:

- Three things you see;
- three things you hear;
- three things you feel.

Feelings can be physical, emotional, or energetic. Take a deep breath and re-engage, more fully present.

Helpful Tip

Try to do this without judgement, of yourself or your surroundings. Don't rush through this. Really noticing what's happening is how this works.

Add a sprinkle of the good

Find something wonderful about yourself, and pay yourself the compliment (in your mind, or even better, out loud!). If someone else is making you crazy, find something genuinely favorable to like about them, too. (You can do this, I promise.)

This isn't trying to cancel out or ignore anything difficult. It's just making a little room for what's good, too. When we make room for what's good, it expands our awareness of the possibilities for more good. Countless scientific studies have shown that positive thinking creates more positive thinking through the creation of new neural pathways. We're not trying to completely rewire our brains in a day, just to think (or say, or write) something nice.

 Helpful Tip

Find yourself having trouble thinking nice thoughts about yourself? Start a note where you jot down the compliments that other people give you. Add to the list whenever you get new compliments and refer back to it often—daily is best.

Positive affirmations

People sometimes make fun of these, but the reason they persist is that they work.

Leave friendly notes for yourself or look in the mirror and say a few loving things. You don't have to believe these things; the more you repeat them to yourself, the truer they will feel.

Try sticking with one or two affirmations for a while; they get more powerful through repetition. Write them down, memorize them, and recite them out loud many times a day. Repeat them silently to yourself during stressful moments. These are your words, and they are powerful.

𝓗𝓮𝓵𝓹𝓯𝓾𝓵 𝓣𝓲𝓹

If you're having trouble thinking of a mantra, try something like this:

I am healthy and happy.

Or,

I am confident and strong, with an open heart and a great sense of humor. I am brimming with confidence and move through the world with ease. I have everything I need, and plenty to share.

Name to tame

Acknowledging something (and naming it) is a big first step toward taming it. Take a deep breath, feel what you are really feeling, and name it.

"Oh, hi, sadness. I see you are here right now."

This isn't welcoming in new things or creating problems, and it's certainly not about beating yourself up about having anxiety, or sadness, or anger, or whatever else you are experiencing. It's about being clear with yourself about your present-moment experience. This allows you to spend your energy dealing with what *is*.

It can be scary to acknowledge what we are feeling because it seems like that might make the emotions "real." The truth is, though, that whatever we are feeling is already real, and admitting these emotions exist begins to take their power away. Rather than enabling feelings to get entrenched, naming them lets them start to move through us; it actually reduces their intensity.

This is an especially good practice for when you feel all mixed up or are acting a certain way but don't know why. We're not trying to change anything; we're just saying hi.

 Helpful Tip

You can even invite the emotions to leave if you want to:
"I acknowledge that you came for a visit, anxiety. I see that you are here right now. But I don't need you right now, and so I invite you to leave."

Message in a bottle

Reach out to someone you haven't seen in ages.

Texting/messaging, cards, emails, e-cards, etc. are all fair game—the goal here is to send genuine warm wishes out into the ether. Pay a compliment or let the person you are reaching out to know why they are meaningful to you.

This is asynchronous communication—you'll send messages out, and they may or may not be returned. That part doesn't matter; the goal is to put some good out there into the world.

Get some affection

Human touch can be a salve to the soul.

If it makes sense, ask someone close to you for a hug. If it doesn't, hug yourself! It releases the same bonding hormone, oxytocin, that you would experience if someone else was hugging you. Give yourself (or someone else) a big squeeze.

Or if you prefer, you can give yourself a moment of affection, such as a gentle hand and wrist massage. This can even be done in the middle of a meeting or class; it will calm you down and help bring yourself back into your own body.

Hand over heart

Put your hand over your heart, close your eyes, and take ten very slow, very deep breaths. Notice how it feels.

Doing this can connect you to your body, it can help to connect you to the emotions you are experiencing, and it can remind you of the power of your physical heart.

The heart has a really strong electromagnetic field (its electrical activity is what an electrocardiogram measures) and because it often works the way it's supposed to, we tend to forget about the incredible amount of energy and life force it is constantly creating for us.

By putting our hands near its energy field and closing our eyes, we can tune in to our hearts in a really powerful way.

---

* *Helpful Tip*

Many ancient traditions believe that the heart chakra is where empathy, love, warmth, and compassion emanate from. What do you feel when you tune in?

TIME: 1 MINUTE

Stranger flings

Say something (genuinely) kind to a stranger. Expect nothing in return, not even acknowledgement. See how it makes you feel. Repeat this as often as possible.

> **Helpful Tip**
>
> It should go without saying, but remember not to be a creep. There's no need to comment on anyone's body, for instance. Stick with things that they chose—like footwear, or kindness.

#010

TIME: 1 MINUTE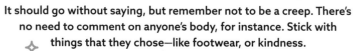

Smile

Even if you don't "mean it," the physical act of smiling releases dopamine, serotonin, and endorphins, which improve our mood and lower our blood pressure. (Smiling also makes us objectively more approachable and attractive.)

Go into a private room, set a timer for sixty seconds and just . . . smile. At the beginning and end of your smile minute, notice how you feel.

Forgive someone

When you find yourself replaying a scenario over and over in your head, you may find it extremely valuable to forgive the person who wronged you (even and especially if that person is you). Visualize the person and repeat: "I forgive you," "I forgive you," "I forgive you."

Even if you don't feel the forgiveness, the suggestion that it's possible can start to do the work.

Repeat as often as needed.

Say the words out loud. Verbalizing can be extremely powerful because when we hear the words out loud, we begin to believe that they are true.

Have a good stretch

Stop, take a few deep breaths, and give yourself a good long stretch.

Try counteracting whatever weird, contorted body position you've been in. Many of us spend a lot of time hunched over desks or computers, so chest-opening stretches feel great; wrist massages can also be sublime.

Find what feels good to you.

Set intentions for the day

Take a deep breath, close your eyes, and think about how you want to be in the world today.

Set an intention around this. It could be something like "Stay present," "Practice kindness," or "Do no harm, but take no shit."

There are no wrong answers; this is about connecting to what feels right to you. Repeat the intention to yourself a few times, really focusing on the words. Take another deep breath, open your eyes, and go about your life with a renewed connection to who you want to be.

This is a particularly effective activity to do when you first wake up in the morning, before getting out of bed or beginning the day.

For inspiration, here are some of my own recent daily intentions:

- ☐ I am present and open to the flow. I feel loved.
- ☐ Relax. Have fun. Be love.
- ☐ I am fully present in my body, open to the flow, and exuding loving gentleness.
- ☐ Today I choose grace and love.

In: nose
Out: mouth

Taking a brief moment to focus on the physical sensations of your breath can be a great way to both reduce heart rate and help you feel more grounded in your own body.

Find a quiet spot if possible, close your eyes, and breathe in slowly and deeply through your nose. Notice the feeling of the air as it passes through your nostrils: the temperature, the taste, and the texture of it. Notice your chest or your stomach rising up as you fill yourself with fresh oxygen. Can you hear yourself breathing?

As you exhale through your mouth, slowly and deeply, notice how your body contracts. Pay attention to whether the qualities of the air moving past your lips are the same, or different, from the air as it came in. Notice again the temperature, taste, and texture of the breath. Exhale slowly and for a long time, until your lungs are emptied out. Pause when it feels natural.

Repeat several times. Go back to breathing normally again, knowing that you can revisit conscious breathing at any time.

✳ *Helpful Tips* ◊

If you can't find a private spot, it's easy to do this one without anyone else knowing it—you can just zone out into your own space.

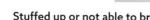

◊ **Stuffed up or not able to breathe through your nose? This exercise works fine if you're breathing through your mouth on both steps.**

Self-commitment appointment

Don't have the time you'd like to devote to yourself right now? Make a self-commitment appointment!

Take one minute right now to commit yourself to a future block of time when you will do nothing but take care of yourself (your future appointment could be for an hour, an afternoon, or a full day; whatever you can make happen).

Get it on your calendar, block it off, and protect it like the precious and important resource that it is. When the occasion comes, you will spend that time doing whatever it is that your body or soul needs in that moment. (Flip through this book for ideas to get you started.)

Self-care is so easy to shove off when more urgent-seeming things come up—but nothing is more important than taking good care of yourself.

3 + h2o

Take three deep, long, beautiful breaths—and then drink a glass of water.

This can be done anytime, anywhere. Don't look at a screen while you do it; close your eyes or look outside. The key is to disconnect from what's outside of your body so that you can reconnect to your most basic physical needs: water and air.

So often we hold our breath without knowing it (lots of people do this while checking email or scrolling through social media), and many of us also unwittingly clench our jaws. Many people also walk through life in a dehydrated state.

So, unclench, breathe deep, and give the 60 percent or so of your body that is water a little boost.

Repeat as often as needed.

Feel your feet

I use this super-fast grounding practice a lot:

Take a deep breath, close your eyes, and feel your feet. Wiggle your toes and maybe rock back and forth on your heels, whatever small movements feel right for you. Then be still and concentrate completely on the feeling of the bottom of your feet touching your shoes or the ground. Breathe slowly and focus on the sensation of the soles of your feet connecting to what's beneath them.

Take another deep breath and return to what's in front of you.

 ### Helpful Tips

If you're sitting, do the same thing while focusing on your bum; if you're lying down, you can repeat this for the part of your body that is being supported. If you're outside, do this barefoot.

This practice is great to do in public; no one will know what you're doing. I especially like this one while I'm stressing out standing in line.

Three things list

Just for today, throw out your overwhelming to-do list and pick the three absolutely most crucial things that must get done. For the rest of the day, only concentrate on those three important things. Everything else can wait! We know this, because none of those made the list as one of the most important things for today.

Make sure they are three things that you can realistically do in one day—*realistically*, I said. If you can't, break them down into smaller and smaller steps until you have three important things that you can definitely get done. Don't set yourself up to fail, set yourself up to succeed!

Bye-bye nonsense

Permanently delete something off of your to-do list.

This isn't punting something until a later date that will likely never come, it's giving yourself permission to let it go completely. Maybe the grout will never get cleaned. Maybe that book will go unread. Maybe holiday cards don't get sent this year.

Chances are, that thing wasn't going to happen anyways, and this practice is about absolving you of feeling guilt; it's a conscious practice in letting go. If you keep saying "I should" about something, that's probably a good thing to get rid of.

Practice saying "No."

"No," as the saying goes, is a complete sentence.

But so often we obscure it with apologies and try to bury it in explanations and excuses and caveats. We walk it back and pretty it up and take the power out of it.

Today, with no apology or explanation, when you mean no . . . just say "No."

50 5-7-8 breaths

Find a quiet place, if possible. Take a deep breath, and as you inhale, slowly count to five. Hold your breath to the count of seven. As you begin to slowly exhale, start counting and make the exhale last until you count to eight.

5
INHALE

7
HOLD

8
EXHALE

Repeat several times, if possible.

This practice connects you to your body, slows down your breathing, and brings your focus inward. It is also a great exercise to do around other people, as no one has to know you are doing it.

Helpful Tip

If it seems interesting, you can work your way up to 8-16-32 counts.

#022

TIME: 1 MINUTE

Stop the "Sorry" madness

Stop apologizing for being human.

There are times when an apology is necessary, but if you, like so many people, apologize dozens of times a day for myriad silly reasons, it's time to stop the madness.

Try stuff like this instead:

~~Sorry I am late.~~

Thanks for waiting for me!

~~Sorry I was so emotional.~~

Thank you for being so supportive and understanding.

~~I am so sorry that I can't do that favor.~~

Thanks for thinking of me! Maybe next time.

~~Sorry it took me so long to reply to that email.~~

Thanks for reaching out.

~~Sorry that I am a human being taking up room in the world.~~

Thanks for holding the door for me.

Square breaths

To do a square breath, think of the four sides of a square made up of your inhale, holding your breath in, your exhale, and holding your breath out. Make them all equal, like the edges of a square.

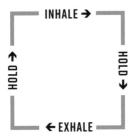

INHALE ➔

HOLD ↑

HOLD ↓

← EXHALE

Start by counting to five on each side and adjust the count to what feels most relaxing to you.

This is especially helpful if you find yourself feeling panicky. By regulating your breathing, you will start to bring your body and your mind back to a place of equanimity.

Helpful Tip

As mentioned in exercise #001, making our exhales longer than our inhales has a direct and immediate effect on our parasympathetic nervous system; it calms us down. Once you've taken a few evenly spaced breaths, count the exhale out for a beat or two longer.

Ear pull

This grounding exercise can help you relax into your body quickly.

With your elbows pointed forward, put your thumbs inside the middle part of your ear, and place your four fingers behind the ear. Gently pull on your ear, in whichever direction and with whatever amount of pressure feels good to you. Do this for a full minute, then end with one slow, deep breath.

Helpful Tip

Another great ear exercise is to rub your palms together until they are warm and place them over your ears. Focus on the feeling of the warmth on your ears for a few moments while you breathe deeply.

"Yes, and . . ."

Buddhism teaches that suffering comes from an attachment to expectations; that we suffer when we want bad things to change (or for good things not to stay the way they are). Improv comedy teaches that the best situations come from accepting what's been presented to us and building on it. Even business leaders are taught this point of view.

The next time you find yourself resistant to something, try the "Yes, and ..." trick: yes, the situation is what it is. And, what's next?

Yes, that jerk cut me off. Yes, the weather sucks. Yes, that horrible person is in charge. Now what? Accepting what's in front of you isn't about liking it or acquiescing to it—it's about seeing the world in front of you plainly for what it is, and then choosing what your next steps are based on how things are and not how you wish they were.

It's a simple, grounding way to be present in the moment, to be fully engaged with what's happening in front of you. Whether you like it or not doesn't matter; it's happening.

Yes, that jerk just cut me off, and instead of flipping the other driver off, I'm going to turn my music up louder and sing along. Yes, this government is failing us, and I'm going to continue to help register people to vote. Yes, this weather sucks, and I'm going to wear bright yellow because someone else probably needs sunshine, too.

The "Yes, and . . ." practice puts your energy where it isn't wasted.

Five-Minute Practices

Carving out a little niche in your day can pay off for you in a big way. In just five minutes you can cause a drastic shift in your perspective. You can change the day's trajectory (or even that of your whole life!), ground down into a feeling of peace, shift up into a higher state of vibration, or really feel the love around and inside of you.

Whether you spend the five minutes disconnecting, reconnecting, or trying something new, it can be time truly well spent. When you are ready for something new, take five.

Alternate nostril
 breathing

In yoga, this exercise is called *Nadi Shodhana*, which in Sanskrit is roughly translated as "flow purification."

Find a relaxed, upright posture. Rest your left hand on your left leg, palm up. Using your right hand, make a "peace sign," and touch those fingers to your forehead. Let your thumb gently touch your right nostril, and let your ring finger and pinkie rest gently on your left nostril.

Breathe in deeply through your nose. Then close your right nostril with your thumb as you exhale through your left nostril. Inhale through your left nostril, then switch fingers: use your pinkie and ring finger to hold your left nostril closed as you exhale, then inhale, through your right nostril. Go for about five minutes (or at least four cycles).

Notice how this exercise affects your body, your emotions, or your thoughts. Take one final deep breath through both sides of your nostrils, then go back to your normal breathing.

✳ *Helpful Tip* ◈

If you start to pay attention to your breathing, you will notice that, at any given time during the day, one nostril is breathing more clearly than the other. (The dominant nostril will change throughout the day.) It is speculated that one reason why this exercise works so well is that it helps oxygenate both sides of the brain.

Enjoy some beauty

The world can sometimes feel like an ugly place, but there is beauty all around.

Take a moment to find something beautiful and enjoy it. The shadows on a building, the sound of someone laughing, the pattern on your dirty car—practice the eye of the artist. You might not find beauty in the first place you look, and this is fine; just keep looking.

We're not trying to separate the beautiful from the sublime here, just to take a brief break from what we think we see, and be open to the gorgeousness that can be found in the mundane. When we look more closely, we might see unexpected patterns, surprising colors, or pleasurable tactile experiences.

Helpful Tips

Sketch what you see, record the sound, or take a picture. Sometimes documenting something can shift the experience even further.

Share the beauty you found with someone else. (I'll admit it, I've been known to invite strangers to smell flowers with me.)

Simple yoga stretches

Yoga isn't just for super-flexible people who can stand on their heads and seem comfortable in pretzel-like contortions. It's for you and me, too!

Look up some simple yoga stretches online and try a few until you find what feels good to you. Here's a simple, restorative pose:

LEGS UP THE WALL POSE

Sit on the floor next to a wall—in any way that makes sense for you— then turn your body so that your back is on the floor and your legs are up the wall. Let your heels rest on the wall with your knees softly bent. (This may not be a graceful transition, but who cares!)

Once your legs are up the wall, customize the pose. Maybe inch your hips closer or further away from the wall. If your chin is higher than your nose, put a pillow behind your head. If it's more comfortable for you, put your legs on a chair, or scoot further away from the wall. Get comfy!

Lie with your legs above your heart for five minutes, or even longer if it's comfortable. When you are done, stand up . . . slowly.

This supported inversion can be calming to the mind, refreshing to the spirit, and kind to the circulation, especially if you are on your feet all day, or sit a lot.

If this pose doesn't feel great, try others!

Mini declutter

Spend five minutes decluttering something that's been bugging you.

Clean out your gym bag, or car trunk, or clear and organize your desk. Wipe down your gross electronics, or finally organize your sock drawer. It doesn't need to turn into a big project; just dive in and declutter. Repeat as desired.

Groom thyself

It's amazing how long we can ignore a painful hangnail, or how many times we'll remind ourselves that we need a haircut appointment but forget to do it.

Whatever that self-grooming thing is that's most needed now, tackle it. Make the dentist appointment, order the electric toothbrush, or look up recipes for a homemade face mask to make at home tonight. Take care of you.

We all feel better when we've taken care of our bodies—and we'll be more relaxed, too. Spend a few minutes caring for your beautiful body.

Make a gratitude list

Everything does not suck.

Make a list of things that are truly good in your life.

Don't overcomplicate it; easy does it. Weather, people, pets, food, you made it to work on time, whatever—if you feel good about it, it's all fair game. See how many you can come up with once you get started. (Even one helps! Hey, you woke up this morning.)

I have a journal that I use just for this, but I also sometimes use a scrap of paper, or a note on my phone. There are a whole host of apps that are designed for this; check some out in the app store if that sounds interesting.

 **𝓗𝓮𝓵𝓹𝓯𝓾𝓵 𝓣𝓲𝓹**

Make it a daily practice.

Make a "to-done" list

Celebrate the small victories in life. It is so easy to get buried under the literally never-ending list of things that we want to get done, but a great way to reframe things is to make a list of all of the things you have already accomplished. When we look at what we've crossed off our proverbial to-do list, we often see only the things that didn't get done; if we look instead at what *did* get accomplished, we'll often find that we did a whole lot more than we realized.

So, make your "to-done" list! List out everything you've gotten done so far today, or this week, or even this year. Be specific and detailed. When you're done making the list, re-read it, and take a moment to really appreciate everything that is on it. You're doing better than you think!

Helpful Tips

A quick trick when making your to-do list is to write down "make a to-do list" as the first item. There, you've already accomplished something! Cross that baby off.

Also, if you're in crisis mode and haven't been knocking them out of the ballpark lately, start your list with "I survived." It really is the most important thing. Your crisis will pass, but the world still needs you. Thank you for surviving.

Do something kind for someone

Doing something kind for someone can measurably make us feel just as good as having someone do something generous for us.

Take five minutes out of your day to look around for, or think up, something compassionate or thoughtful that you can do for someone else—and do it.

You could pay for someone's expired parking meter, help someone carry packages, pick up some trash. Maybe you tape $1 to the office vending machine, learn how to say "hello" in the native language of someone in your life, or let a harried stranger skip ahead of you in line. You could do an extra household chore or errand, buy someone a treat, or drive with extra courtesy today.

The specific act of kindness doesn't matter, and neither does the outcome: we're just setting out to spend five minutes today doing a little good. Do this without expectation of thanks or reward; the service itself is the practice.

> "If you want others to be happy, practice compassion. If you want to be happy, practice compassion."
>
> **DALAI LAMA**

Treat yourself to a beautiful game on your phone

Phones aren't inherently bad; there is beauty to be found in them, too.

Many of us find that we've picked up our phones without even knowing why and we end up scrolling through social media or reading the news, both of which tend to make us feel bad. While later practices in the book address cutting back on phone time, this one is about shifting the behavior.

Find and download a beautiful game to play on your phone. Next time you're tempted to mindlessly scroll through social media or check the news, open one of your favorite game apps instead.

Helpful Tip

Wear headphones—the music is part of the experience of many of these stunning pieces of playable art.

Note to self

Who deserves your love and affection more than you? No one! Give it up for yourself!

Write yourself a beautiful letter about the things you love, appreciate, and admire about yourself. (Yes, this will feel weird, but forget about that.) What do you wish the voices in your head said? Write it down. Remind yourself that you are a strong, beautiful, and worthy human being. Detail why. Be generous and expansive.

Make this a real letter: greetings and salutations, date it, stamp it, and put it in the mail. When you receive it, re-read it with fresh eyes.

Helpful Tip

Make this a monthly practice. Gather the letters in a special place and revisit them when you need a boost. While relationships with others matter immensely, the most important voice in your life is yours. This is an opportunity to make it a kind one.

Acupressure

There are lots of acupressure points that do many different, wonderful things for our bodies. Here's one that I've found works really well for me.

The meaty spot on your hand, right between your pointer finger and your thumb, is referred to in acupuncture as point LI4 (large intestine 4). It is a trigger point for the fascia (connective tissue) that is connected to our necks and jaws. When we pinch, hold, or massage this spot, we are promoting mental clarity and relieving tension from our digestive system, from our neck and jaw, and from overuse of our hands and wrists. Rub or massage it in whatever way feels good to you. Try using a little essential oil, too, if that sounds nice. I find that massaging this spot can be fantastic for relieving headaches.

If you don't love this spot, or if you do love it and want to try other areas of the body, look up additional simple acupressure spots online. (If you're pregnant or breastfeeding, talk to an expert before trying acupressure or using essential oils.)

Dream big . . . backwards

Spend some time thinking about a big, seemingly impossible dream that you have. Starting a business, traveling the world, doing a triathlon—whatever you've been secretly dreaming about. Make a "dream big backwards" list. Start with the achievement of your dream, and list back all of the things you'll have to do to get there. If your dream is to travel the world, it might be something like:

1. Make reservations.

2. Research itinerary.

3. Save up enough money.

4. Start travel savings account.

5. Get passport.

And so on. Once you've worked all the way backwards, set up a time to do the closest, easiest, smallest step. In this case, it might be to print out a passport form, for example. Then the next step might be to log into your bank account and move a few bucks into a new savings account. Just start—and set up a regular time to keep taking these baby steps. It's how dreams are accomplished!

Change the actual air

Many of us spend the majority of our days (both the waking and the sleeping hours) breathing indoor air. Indoor air, in many parts of the world, is less healthy for us than outdoor air. According to the Environment Protection Agency, in the US indoor air is two to five times more polluted than outdoor air.

Breathing clean, fresh air can boost your immune system, the higher concentrations of oxygen can improve our brain health, and it helps our lungs dilate more fully. Fresh air is filled with negative ions, which naturally clean the air. (Think of the awesome feeling in the air near a big waterfall or after a storm—that's negative ions, and they are so good for us that people buy ionizers for the home.)

Just the smell of nature has been shown to help us feel calmer, while fresh oxygen actually energizes us. Calm energy—we could all use more of that! If you live in an urban area, breathing fresh air—especially that around nature (trees clean the air naturally)—can be especially important. If you live or work in a crowded place, you are probably contending with a lot of germs, too.

So, ready for something new?

Open the windows. Or go outside and breathe deeply. Drive with the car windows rolled down. If you are lucky enough to live where the fresh air is abundant, soak it up!

Or if you are stuck inside (or live in a polluted place), take the five minutes to order a HEPA air filter, or to explore natural air filters (such as activated charcoal, plants, beeswax candles, or salt lamps).

Changing the air you breathe for the better will change your health (mental and physical!) for the better, too.

#039

TIME: 5 MINUTES

Leave five minutes earlier

Leave for (or start something) five minutes earlier than usual.

Take a different route, give yourself more time to think before you get started on a project, or just let the moment at hand expand to fill the space.

Too often we are rushing from one thing to another, scrambling to get from one place to the next, and trying to squeeze too few things into not enough time. We become completely acclimated to the crunch, forgetting even how the alternatives feel.

No pressure for a huge lifestyle shift, just start your next task or trip five minutes earlier and see how it feels.

#040

TIME: 5 MINUTES

Sing it

Sing a song at the top of your lungs!

Or if you can't do that, blast a song on your headphones, close your eyes, and soak up the music. Just enjoy the music and let it transport you. Don't worry about how you sound or what you look like, this is about how you feel.

Explore essential oils

Essential oils can have myriad benefits, ranging from increased immunity to better sleep, enhanced focus, easier digestion, and lowered inflammation (depending on the type of oil and its quality). Any health store has dozens of essential oils to choose from; take a few minutes to sniff them out and find one or two that appeal to you.

Peppermint, lemon, and eucalyptus are uplifting; lavender, chamomile, and ylang-ylang are relaxing. Tea tree is naturally antibacterial, and ginger is surprisingly good at helping with nausea. But don't overthink it; whatever you are drawn to is the right choice.

Integrate it into your life: put a few drops into unscented lotion and use it to moisturize yourself, put a drop on your wrist (if the bottle says that's okay), add some to your shower, or put a few drops on unscented baby wipes and put them in a baggie to use later (or go the old-fashioned route and add a few drops to a handkerchief!).

Notice how the oil makes you feel. If you like it, explore more aromas! (If you're pregnant or breast feeding, talk to an expert before using essential oils.)

Helpful Tip ✳

If you find that you really like using essential oils, consider buying a diffuser for your home, car, or office.

Self-love list

I would be willing to bet that if I asked you to, you could quickly come up with a list of things you don't like about yourself. (I know that my own personal "self-loathe" list lives pretty close to the surface.)

Please know that this isn't a personal character flaw, to not like parts of yourself—and it certainly does not mean that there is anything actually wrong with you. In today's society, where "self-improvement" masks itself as "wellness," and the idea that we have to "work on ourselves" or even "be better" has become part of popular culture, we are inundated with the idea that there is always something we need to improve. Eff that.

We're going to take a few minutes to start to flip this idea on its head. Introducing . . . the self-love list!

Take five minutes, right now, to start and keep a running list of things you love about yourself.

Anything you like is fair game: your personality, your character, your creativity, your values, your choices. Bonus if something about your physical body is on the list—and double bonus if something about what your body *does* instead of how it looks makes the cut.

 Helpful Tip

Spread the love and share your list! Loving yourself visibly is a radical act these days.

TIME: 5 MINUTES

Mindful eating

In the same way that we can take a moment to more mindfully enjoy a drink (see #050), we can also pay close attention to our next bites of food. Either spend five minutes enjoying a snack or spend an extra five minutes at the beginning of a meal, fully engaging all of your senses.

Take the time to notice:

- ☒ How does this food look?
- ☒ Who took part in growing it and packaging it and getting it to me?
- ☑ What happens in my body when I look at this food?
- ☑ When I put it in my mouth, what is the first taste like?
- ☑ What is the texture of the food?
- ☑ Do I crave more immediately or do I feel sated?
- ☑ What else is noticeable?

Really observe your body's response to the food.

When we choose to eat more mindfully, we naturally eat less, make healthier food choices, and digest better. (Doing things like driving or watching TV while we eat can put our body into fight-or-flight mode, during which digestion shuts down. Better digestion means we get more nutrients from our foods.)

Mindful eating helps us tune in to what our bodies really want, and when we do that, we're much better equipped to take good care of ourselves. It can also help our food taste better. The practice is simple, but the benefits are great!

Diaphragmatic breathing

Many of us tend to take shallow breaths into our chests. This constricts our breathing and can trigger the fight-or-flight response that keeps our bodies in stress mode. When we do diaphragmatic (deep, low) breathing, we are instead focusing on bringing the entire breath deeper into our bodies.

Start by lying down, if possible. Place one hand on your chest and one on your upper belly. To practice diaphragmatic breathing: take a deep breath in through your nose, and as you do, fill up your belly with air. As you exhale through your mouth, notice your belly contracting. Pay attention to the sensation of your belly rising and falling.

Your chest will ideally remain relatively still, as our upper bellies rise and fall, rise and fall, with slow, deep breaths.

Doing this practice daily can start to reduce your overall stress levels in as little as two weeks.

> ### *Helpful Tip* ✳
>
> **The practice goes well with music or even a calm show.**

Tense & relax

This exercise is also called Progressive Muscle Relaxation, or PMR. To do this practice, you are going to concentrate on tensing, and then relaxing, different muscles.

Lie down in a quiet place if you can. You can do this in any order you like, but you might consider starting with the feet and moving up your body in an order like this: feet, lower legs, upper legs, rear, stomach, chest, back, hands, arms, shoulders, neck, mouth, eyes, and then forehead.

Starting with the first muscle you chose, as you inhale, squeeze it as tight as you can. FEEL the tension. Ball up the muscle, making it as tight as you comfortably can. Hold, hold, hold!

Now relax the muscle as you exhale. Observe how it feels after releasing the tension. Pay close attention; don't skip this part. The aim is to notice the difference in the feelings and sensations when your muscles are tensed up versus relaxed, so give yourself the time to observe that.

It's okay if the tension makes you shaky—just as long as it doesn't hurt. If you have injuries or are worried, talk to your doctor first.

Work your way up (or down) your entire body, taking as much time as you can. When you are finished, spend one last moment feeling the sensation of all of your muscles being relaxed. (If you have any existing tension, exhale through it.)

 Helpful Tip

✧ **This practice is especially nice for children before bedtime.**

Five-minute dance party!

Find a private spot (a room, your car, the bathroom), pick a song you love, and have a five-minute personal dance party!

Combining the escapism of focusing on the music with the benefits of physical movement will leave you feeling refreshed and reinvigorated. It's a great way to change up how you're feeling.

Do this in private or with people (such as kids or kind colleagues) who will not care what you look like. Close your eyes, feel the music, and move your body. How you move doesn't matter—you can be mostly paralyzed or the best dancer on planet Earth and you can still bust out some kind of moves.

Use headphones if it feels more private. Sing along if you feel like it. Try to move your body (or some part of it) for the entirety of a song. Slow, fast, standing, sitting, lying on the floor or a sofa, hips, legs, arms, head, whatever . . . just move to the music.

Helpful Tip

Don't know what song to try? Start with "En Love" by Lizzo, or "Love Me Now" by John Legend.

TIME: 5 MINUTES

Delegate something

Don't try to do everything yourself. Get some help!

Arrange for someone else to handle a task (or many tasks!) from your to-do list. Look for help from a friend, a spouse, or a partner; if you have the funds available, you can even hire some help through an online service.

Many of us loathe asking for help but are happy to offer it to others. This is the time to flip that on its head. Don't stress about it, and don't beat yourself up about it, just get some help.

Is getting help not the right answer? See practice #019.

#048

TIME: 5 MINUTES

Just. Take. A. Break.

Take a five-minute break. Seriously, just walk away from whatever is stressing you out.

Take five minutes to focus on literally anything else, which gives you the space you deserve to let yourself calm down and start to think clearly.

Take the whole five minutes; don't take two and then dive back in. Add some deep breathing or stretching if it feels right.

Tech five

Today, only check news, social media, and your email inbox at designated times. Give yourself five minutes for each (or whatever period of time makes sense—but be sure to time it and stick to it). The endless scrolling and constant refreshing that many of us engage in sucks up enormous amounts of time. By designating certain times, you can check in guilt-free but you won't lose yourself in the constant temptation.

This can help you not feel so dependent on your devices, it can reduce stress, and it's beneficial to both your physical and your mental health. And, it will help you get more done during the day. Bonus!

Helpful Tip
Try using apps that tell you how much time you spend on your phone. Knowledge is power!

Have a drink

Take five minutes to enjoy—really enjoy—a beverage: tea, coffee, some fizzy water, whatever sounds good to you. Enjoy the ritual of getting it ready and pay attention to the way the first sip feels going down. What is the temperature of the drink? Where do you taste it on your tongue? Does it smell the same as it tastes? Set a timer and spend five minutes doing nothing but hydrating and enjoying the way it feels to carve out a little time to simply enjoy your drink.

If possible, physically go to a new space—outside is great, or standing up near a window if you've been sitting down all day, or in a private break room, or in your car. No screens, no books, no conversation: just you, taking five to enjoy your drink of choice.

Helpful Tip

It's probably best not to down an alcoholic bevvie in five minutes. But . . . you can still really enjoy your next cocktail in a similar way, albeit more slowly. Engage in a little bit of mindful drinking!

TIME: 5 MINUTES

Write a poem

Grab a pen and a piece of paper and set a timer for five minutes. It's time to write a poem!

This practice will pique your creativity, take you out of your set patterns of thinking, and maybe even spark a little fun.

In case it's been a while since you've written a poem, here are some types you could choose from (although anything counts):

- Acrostic (the beginning letters of each line spell something).
- Limericks (five lines, A-A-B-B-A rhyming).
- Haiku (three lines, 5-7-5 syllables).
- Narrative (tells a story).
- Shape (the words form a shape of something talked about in the poem).
- Sonnet (14-line poem with varying rhymes, and each line has 10 syllables).
- Free verse (no rules!).

Having trouble getting started? Look around and write the poem about something that catches your eye.

Helpful Tip

I love how the meditation teacher and author Adreanna Limbach often uses poetry as her Instagram captions. Check her out for inspiration!

Laugh!

Laughter can be incredible medicine, truly.

A good laugh can relieve stress, release endorphins, stimulate circulation, relax our muscles, lower our blood pressure, and increase our oxygen intake. Laughter is a natural painkiller, it can help lessen anxiety and depression, and over time it can even improve our immune systems. (And you thought it was just fun!)

Seek out some funny stuff: you can search for funny YouTube videos, read books like *Stuff on My Mutt* by Mario Garza, look up jokes online, or find joke books at the library. If you like stand-up comedy, explore some of the many Netflix comedy specials (but only watch as long as they make you feel good; we're not going for cringeworthy here, we're seeking Laugh Out Loud-worthy).

When you find something funny, bookmark it for later. Ask other people what makes them laugh. Heck, start a laugh collection! When you find something really makes you laugh, make a note of it, and refer back to it when you need a pick-me-up.

Helpful Tip ✳

Looking for a place to start? I recommend Jess Rona's Grooming Instagram account; the behind-the-scenes pics of her dog grooming business are too much—in a good way. The comedy specials of Trevor Noah and Eddie Izzard are faves of mine, too.

Twenty-Minute Practices

When we are able to devote a little more time, we can make some meaningful changes. Whether it's through a power nap or a full meditation session, a mini-remodel or a few chapters of a book, we can really take ourselves out of the fray and very meaningfully refocus where our energy is going.

It can sometimes be a bit of a challenge to commit this amount of time to self-care—there is always something that feels more urgent—but doing what it takes to grab those ten (or hopefully twenty!) minutes out of the day is a huge step in taking care of you. When the struggle is real, fight back by claiming some time for yourself.

Take a nap (or rest) break

Twenty minutes is enough time to get in a power nap—but for a lot of people, we're not able to just lie down and sleep.

If you are able to nap, DO IT!

If you are not a napper, find a quiet spot (an empty meeting room, your car, a bench) and put on some soothing music through your headphones. Close your eyes and just . . . relax. If you, like me, are worried about time, set a gentle alarm so that you don't fret about it.

If you find yourself stressing out, picture yourself placing the worries at the end of the nap time. They'll still be there, you're just not engaging with them for a few moments. And by all means, don't place any undue pressure on yourself to fall asleep. If you can sleep, awesome, but resting is enough.

Get some sunshine

Millions of us suffer from vitamin D deficiency, and the medical establishment is just starting to understand how widespread the problem is. The US National Institutes of Health says that "vitamin D insufficiency affects almost 50 percent of the population worldwide." This can lead to fatigue, pain, and a loss of bone density—which is especially scary as we age. As humans, we are made to be outside, but instead so many of us spend most (or virtually all!) of our time inside, basking in the glow of light bulbs instead of the sun's rays.

Spending ten to twenty minutes a day soaking up the sunshine can make an enormous difference to your short-term mood, as well as help prevent long-term side effects such as vitamin D deficiency (which can lead to heart disease) and a weakened immune system.

So, soak up some rays! And if it isn't sunny, consider getting a full-spectrum lamp, which is a good sunlight substitute. I suffer terribly from Seasonal Affective Disorder (SAD) and find that sitting in front of my "blue light" is a daily occurrence during the dark winter months.

Helpful Tip

Those of us worried about skin cancer tend to slather on the sunscreen, but this also blocks out the vitamin D that our bodies need. Talk to your doctor about finding the right amount of time to spend in the sun (and, the darker your skin, the more time in the sun you'll want to aim for).

Feel the water

Being in, or even near, natural bodies of water can induce relaxation; cause a mild meditative state; lower levels of stress, anxiety, and depression; and improve focus. It also helps boost creativity; we've all had those *eureka!* moments in the shower.

This practice is about spending a dedicated amount of time in water—with no screens or other distractions. If it's available to you, by all means go for a dip in the ocean or a lake! But if that's not a possibility, choose another way to get water onto your body: go for a swim in a pool, sit in a hot tub, or take a warm shower or bath.

Whatever you choose to do, once you are immersed, focus on feeling the water: its viscosity, temperature, and texture. Is it calm or choppy? Does it flow, drip, or swell? What does it feel like as it is moving past your skin? Is it all one color or different shades? Does it have a unique scent?

There is no judgement, and there are no right or wrong answers. Our aim is to focus on the feeling of the water, however it manifests itself in the moment. Just swim in the feelings, whatever they are.

✳

Helpful Tips

Even a brief moment of splashing water on your face or on your wrists is enough to receive some of the calming benefits of water. If you're stressed out, go to the restroom and splash a little on yourself while you take a deep breath.

✦   ✦

Spend one minute of every shower just feeling the water on your body.

Write a letter

Compose a letter to someone telling them how much they mean to you, and why.

This can be someone in your personal life, family, past, career network, an author whose work you love, or anyone whose influence you have appreciated.

If it's to someone who has passed away or is otherwise unreachable, you can still write it—and then you can keep it—or send it to someone who will treasure knowing that their loved one's memory lives on.

Notice how this makes you feel. Does it surprise you? If you decide to repeat this practice, pay attention to how writing to different people, or about different things, makes you feel.

Helpful Tip

Handwritten notes, if you are able to do them, are a beautiful and deeply personal way to communicate what's in your soul.

Move the room

Sometimes all that's needed for a new perspective is . . . a new perspective. Take a few moments to really switch up something in your life. Rearrange the furniture in one room in your home (or at your office). Don't worry about whether you will love it or not; you can move it back if you don't.

The point is to shake things up a little bit and remind yourself that there are always options, even in the tiniest parts of our lives and routines. Invite some change into your life in a physical and real way.

Not yet ready to rearrange the room? Spend the time putting together a completely original outfit, perhaps, or totally change the way a bookshelf is arranged, or how some artwork is displayed.

Pay attention to how it all feels: the decision, the process, and the result. Do you like the change? Do you feel open to it or closed off? Does the change manifest in your body anywhere, or cause you to want to lean in or move away? As always, no judgements here, just observations and information.

✦ *Helpful Tip* ◆

Try applying this idea in other areas of your life as well. Maybe you take a completely new route to somewhere you frequently go. Maybe you do a little drawing with your non-dominant hand. Don't worry at all about the outcome, we're just trying a new process here.

Enjoy some fiction

Choose and start a classic fiction book.

With good fiction comes escapism. While reading business books or the news might keep you informed, reading fiction helps us disengage in a really healthy way.

Reading fiction helps us to develop empathy, sleep better, and aids in stress reduction. It increases our own creativity and open-mindedness, builds our vocabulary, and slows memory decline. Reading fiction can help put our minds into a trancelike state, similar to meditation, and helps our minds make new connections.

Don't save fiction just for vacations—it's one of the best ways you can spend your time.

If you love the book you chose, explore other books by the same author or in the same genre. If you don't love it, put it down and try another one!

Helpful Tip

Expand your view! Seek out books by authors who come from underrepresented cultures and backgrounds. There's gold to be found when looking outside of the typical suspects. If you're not sure where to start, you could check out the works of Paulo Coelho de Souza, Toni Morrison, Kevin Kwan, Min Jin Lee, or Chinua Achebe.

Journal

Journaling, even occasionally, can help you heal, spark your creative mind, reduce stress, and help you get to know yourself better.

Find or buy a beautiful notebook and pen. Choose from one of the following practices and spend ten to twenty minutes writing.

- ☑ Free writing: start with the first thing that comes to mind, and don't stop writing until the time is up.
- ☑ Do a "Dear Diary" entry where you talk about your day.
- ☑ Make a gratitude list (see #031).
- ☑ Make a list of hopes, goals, or dreams.
- ☑ Create a progress report about existing goals.
- ☑ Write down something funny that happened to you.
- ☑ Compose a reflection (essentially, a story about your past).

If this resonated with you, make it a regular practice! Daily journaling has many long-term mental health benefits, like reducing feelings of depression and anxiety, improving memory, and boosting your mood.

 Helpful Tip

This is for you, and you alone. Don't worry about grammar, spelling, or what anyone else would think. No editing needed; just write.

Phone a friend

Call someone you know to be reliably kindhearted, just to say hello. It could be a parent, an old friend, or a new love interest. If no one comes to mind, consider someone whose day may be brightened by your call—an elderly relative, or a friend you know is going through a tough time.

This isn't the moment to think about whom you "should" call; the point of this is to reach out and directly connect to someone who makes you feel good, or whom you can make feel good. Don't worry about obligations or wish that someone in your life would be more reliably kind; just make a thoughtful connection with someone you can count on.

Helpful Tips

Can't bear to call? Send a text, a DM, a Snap or WeChat, or whatever. Not everyone loves to talk on the phone. The most important thing is to take the first step in reaching out. Open yourself up and connect with someone kind.

Couldn't get a hold of someone, or they were distracted, rushed, or otherwise not as able to connect as you'd hoped? It's not you, and it's fine. Just try someone else.

Enter explorer mode

Oftentimes, falling into the proverbial online rabbit hole is a distraction, but sometimes diving deeply into the unknown is just what we need.

Open up Wikipedia, or better yet, visit a library, and read about . . . well, anything that interests you. As you read, give yourself permission to explore other topics as they come up. Tangents welcome!

Not sure where to start? Recent topics that have fascinated me are Fordlândia, the Suez Canal, Amazonian river dolphins, and the Cortes Bank seamount. Try one of those, or just start browsing.

The key here is to let your mind wander and see where it leads. So often we associate a wandering mind with distraction, or a lack of discipline, or a waste of time, but a wandering mind can be a creative, imaginative, open one. So let's cultivate that!

✳ *Helpful Tip* ◈

For this exercise, try to avoid highly charged emotional topics. The point of this one is to stimulate your intellectual curiosity.

Body scan

Doing a body scan can help us to ground into our bodies, connect to the present moment, reduce tension, and alleviate stress.

To do a body scan:

1. Lie down comfortably in a quiet spot where you won't be interrupted; close your eyes and take a few deep breaths.

2. Check in with yourself; notice how you're feeling (without judgement or a need to fix).

3. Use your awareness to scan the body, spending a moment focusing on each place, simply noticing how the body feels.

4. When observing how you feel, you might notice things like temperature, tension or relaxation, tingling, hardness or softness, and many more sensations.

5. Move up your body, spending time in each spot to notice how it feels.

6. Perhaps try this order: feet, lower legs, upper legs, rear, stomach, chest, hands, arms, shoulders, neck, mouth, eyes, and then forehead.

7. When your mind wanders, simply bring it back without admonishing yourself.

8. Engage a sense of curiosity: we're not judging or changing, simply noticing.

9. At the end of the scan, take a few more deep breaths. Open your eyes and return to your day.

TIME: 20 MINUTES

Meditate

Meditation can be intimidating to try, but the benefits have been studied copiously by scientists and are, frankly, incredible. With a regular meditation practice, we can reduce our stress and anxiety, get better sleep, and actually start to rewire the gray matter in our brain—in as little as eight weeks. There are many types of meditation, and many routes in. Try a few different things until you find what works for you.

To do a simple mindfulness–awareness (*shamatha*) meditation:

- ☑ Find a quiet place where you won't be interrupted.
- ☑ Get into a comfortable, upright position (a cushion or a chair are both great; just aim to have your knees below your hips).
- ☑ Place your hands gently on your legs (without gripping) and gently close your eyes.
- ☑ Take a moment to check in with how you feel, without judgement.
- ☑ Take a few slow, deep breaths.
- ☑ Pay attention to the physical sensation of the breath entering and leaving your body.
- ☑ When your mind wanders, notice that, then gently bring your attention back to the breath.
- ☑ Repeat the above step over and over again, until the time is up.
- ☑ Before you finish, take one last moment to check in with how you're feeling.
- ☑ Take a few more deep breaths and open your eyes.

You meditated! If, even once, you noticed that your mind was wandering and then brought your attention back to the breath, you practiced mindfulness. It's not clearing the mind of all thought that makes it mindfulness, it's noticing when the mind wanders.

If a self-guided meditation doesn't feel right, you can try one of the dozens of meditation apps or thousands of recorded meditations online. (They vary in quality, so be sure to look at reviews.) Many big cities (and even smaller ones) now have drop-in meditation studios, sanghas (meditation communities), or meditation classes held at yoga studios.

5 RULES FOR MEDITATION BEGINNERS

1. When you first meditate, it can be incredible to discover how loud your mind is. This is normal.

2. You can't meditate "wrong" or be bad at it. It's a practice.

3. Sticking with it daily (ten to twenty minutes) can create incredible change.

4. Try different stuff until you find what works!

5. The most important thing—always!—is to be gentle with yourself.

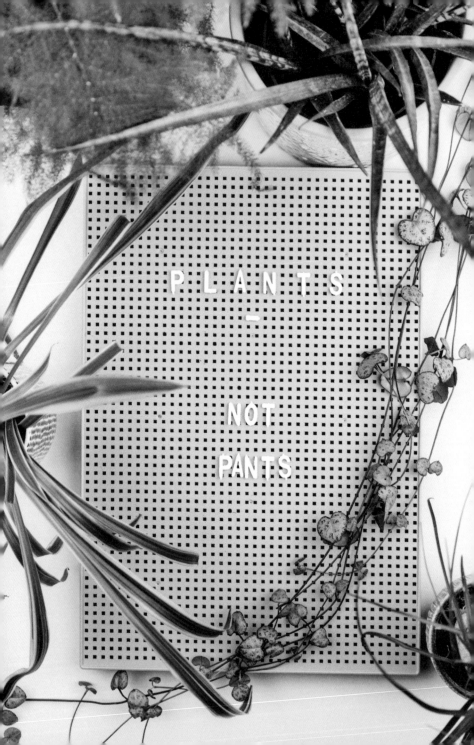

Bring some ~~well~~
nature inside

We can't always get outside as much as we'd like, but we can bring the outdoors in. Spend a little bit of time finding a way to invite nature into your home or workspace.

You could:

1. Change your computer background and phone lock screen to a nature scene that inspires you.

2. Take some things you've gathered from outside (maybe even on a nature walk, **exercise #084**) and spread them throughout your workspace.

3. Start a "nature shelf" in your house where you display your treasures from outside.

4. Put a few rocks into a small bowl on your desk to play with while you work.

5. Buy sustainably grown cut flowers for your home—for an even greater impact, divide the flowers among small glasses and place them in every room of your house.

6. Hang a picture of nature where you wish a window was (such as in your cubicle)—there's no need to spend money on this if you don't want to; peruse some magazines and tear out a great picture.

There are no rules, other than doing whatever makes you feel good. Connecting to nature is one of the best things you can do for your health, but you don't have to wait until you get outside to do it.

Give guilt the day off

Enjoy the crap out of a normally guilty pleasure.

Give yourself permission, just this once, to drop the guilt when it comes up. You can always feel guilty later—right now is for pure pleasure.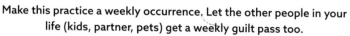

A giant bowl of Cheetos and an episode of your favorite show? Dreamy. Dig in.

Helpful Tip   ✦

Make this practice a weekly occurrence. Let the other people in your life (kids, partner, pets) get a weekly guilt pass too.

Each school year when my daughter was young, I gave her a "hooky day" pass, where she could skip school once, with no excuse needed. I figure that we all deserve mental health days. Maybe the kids in your life could benefit from the same?

Unsubscribe party!

Your email inbox is your digital home; keep it clean and only let people hang out there who you really want around you.

Spend some time unsubscribing from every email list that you don't absolutely love. What lands in your inbox ought to be personal messages or things that make you feel good. Sale flyers, newsletters you subscribed to out of obligation, social media websites whining for attention, marketing lists you never asked to be on to begin with, summaries of all the bad news in a day . . . get rid of it all. Be ruthless!

Helpful Tip ✳

If you have the interest, many mail programs have in their advanced settings ways for you to set up different "rules" for email. If you want to keep getting discount codes from a shopping site, for example, you can set up a rule that it will skip the inbox. That way, you can search for it if you need to, but it won't eat up your valuable attention.

(Note: Do NOT use mass unsubscribing tools. They sell your personal information to the highest bidder. It's much better to do the work yourself.)

Thirty-Minute
Practices

When five or twenty minutes is good, half an hour can be even better. This is enough time that we can go a little deeper: into nature, into ourselves, into our bodies, or into our intentions. When it seems tempting to skip the middle ground between a quick five- or ten-minute practice and the deeper hour-plus exercises, try some of these medium-sized gems.

It's easy to spend a half hour scrolling on social media, zoning out to Netflix, or spacing out at work. No shame, but every once in a while, try one of these practices instead. When you do, pay attention to how you feel at the end of it compared to how you feel after your typical zone-out-of-choice. You might notice that there's room for some more intentional half-hour time blocks in your life.

TIME: 30 MINUTES

Earthing

Many of us are nearly completely disconnected from the rhythms of nature, and this is taxing to our bodies and our emotional health. Any time that we spend connecting with nature has incredible physical and mental health benefits.

The practice of earthing, or grounding, is about using our physical bodies to connect directly with nature. You know that feeling of taking off your shoes and rubbing your toes through the grass, or digging your feet into the sand? It feels awesome! That's earthing.

So get yourself into nature, somewhere that you can relax and feel comfortable for a half hour. Once you've settled into your spot, take your shoes off and feel the ground with your feet. Breathe deeply, and focus first on the physical sensations in your feet: how does the ground feel? What is the texture? The temperature? Concentrate for a few minutes on how it feels. If you feel restless during your half hour of grounding, feel free to read a book (no screens!) or even go for a barefoot walk.

Other ways to connect directly to the Earth are sitting or lying on the ground (read a book or have a picnic), gardening, hugging a tree, or going for a swim in a natural body of water. The point is to have your physical body connect directly to the Earth, without shoes or windows in the way.

This practice is similar to exercises **#078 (Forest bathing)** and **#098 (Take a hike)**, but our main focus when earthing, or grounding, is to get our bodies into *direct* contact with the Earth. It doesn't have to be complicated or weird. Our bodies will often naturally lead us into what is good for us if we let them.

Take a podcast walk

Friends, we are in the golden age of podcasts—there are so many! And while a lot of people enjoy multitasking while listening to them (I love to listen to them while I clean), the act of really focusing on them can be very meditative. ~~we could read these~~

So, find a podcast that uplifts or inspires you, and take it for a walk. Put your phone into airplane mode, pop on some headphones, and just set out. Really immerse yourself in what you're hearing, and before you know it, it will be time to turn around.

Helpful Tips

Storytelling podcasts are best for this because they let you truly go deep. If you don't already have favorite podcasts, ask your friends for recommendations.

Can't walk, or too exhausted today? Have a sit and enjoy the podcast instead.

Soup

Yes, that's it: soup.

Soup is comfort food in a huge variety of cultures and it comes in a bazillion variations. Soup is delicious, a great way to eat more veggies, is filling and often high in fiber, and those with broth bases are rich in vitamins and essential minerals. Choose your favorite, most comforting kind and make (or order) it for your next meal.

For me, it's chicken pho with an egg in it; for my husband, it's either borscht or ramen; for my mom, it's lentil soup. If it's hot outside, make a gazpacho or a vichyssoise. If you're vegetarian, you might want a black bean or butternut squash soup. If you're a meat lover, you might try an Italian wedding or vegetable beef stew. Go for whatever makes your mouth water.

If you don't have the desire or time to make soup, buy it ready-made or order it from your favorite restaurant. Serve it with some crusty bread and good company or a good book.

Just . . . take some time to enjoy every mouthful.

Do a deep clean

Set a timer for thirty minutes and spend that time doing a deep clean of something that's been bugging you.

It can be physical cleaning: the junk drawer, that huge pile of paperwork, the houseplants that need refreshing. Or it can be a digital cleanup: clean out your inbox, update your contacts lists, or finally change those weak passwords you've been meaning to update.

The point is to keep your cleaning project finite (don't let it snowball into something too big to finish) and to relieve some minor, low-grade stress from your life.

Play a game on paper

Playing games on our devices can be fun (my husband will tell you that I've spent countless hours doing this), but there's nothing quite like playing a game on paper.

Buy a book of games or find free versions online and print them out. Choose whatever piques your interest: I like crossword puzzles and Sudoku myself; other people I know love mazes, logic puzzles, or adult coloring books. You could even grab a deck of cards and play (offline) solitaire. As long as it's on physical paper, it's fair game.

Salt bath

One of my favorite truisms was stated by the writer Isak Dinesen (actually the Baroness Karen Blixen writing under a pseudonym).

"The cure for anything is salt water—sweat, tears, or the sea."

I believe this wholeheartedly. And for those of us who don't have the sea outside our front doors, salt baths can be the perfect way to go. Salt water is detoxifying, rejuvenating, and can induce a state of deep relaxation.

Different salts have different benefits: Epsom salts are high in magnesium, replenish electrolytes, and balance hormones; Dead Sea salt is particularly good for the skin; and mineral-rich pink Himalayan salt can help improve hydration and maintain the pH balance of the body. All salt baths help us relax, ease muscle aches, and get better sleep.

Don't have a bathtub? Salt scrubs are the way to go. You can easily make your own from coarse sea salt mixed with coconut or olive oil. If you'd like, add a few drops of the essential oil of your choice.

Helpful Tip
The more salt you add to a bath, the longer the temperature of the water will be maintained.

Try a longer, guided meditation

While meditating for ten minutes a day can start to have a big impact on your mind-set, meditating for longer amounts of time can do even more for your well-being. It can be intimidating to commit to this amount of time if you're not used to it, though, so a good way to try a longer session is with a guided meditation.

The point is to explore deeper meditation, and to see whether it might be something that you'd like to integrate into your life more regularly. If you don't like it, totally fine. If you do find some you like, consider doing them more often and for longer. Meditating for longer amounts of time regularly can result in deep, long-lasting benefits.

✳ *Helpful Tip*

You can check out more guided meditations, there are a ton available online (including many free ones on YouTube, (although they vary wildly in quality), or check out some meditation apps that offer guided meditation.

Leave a half hour early

So often we rush, rush, rush. It's stressful, it's predictable, and yet it happens far more often than we would like.

The next time you have somewhere to be, leave half an hour early. (A full half hour, don't spend fifteen minutes finishing up a household chore and then leave fifteen minutes early; leave a full half hour before you normally would.)

What will you do with the time? Who knows?! Just see what happens. Do you arrive early and have some time to relax? Do you make a pleasant stop somewhere along the way? Do you just slow down and enjoy the journey a little bit more? Do you take the scenic route?

I made a commitment to myself to leave early as often as I can. I realized that I don't like how I act when I am rushed: not holding doors, shoving my way onto a crowded subway car, feeling annoyed when someone tries to make light conversation. This isn't how I want to be in the world, and so I consciously try to avoid it when I can.

During your half hour, notice: How do you feel? Is it different from how you normally feel? Is your body less tense? Does your breathing change? No judgement; we're just noticing. If it feels good, consider making it a more regular practice.

Social media makeover

Your social media feeds are *your* personal space. Spend half an hour actively unfollowing (or muting) anyone who doesn't make you feel good about yourself and your life. Set a timer and don't get distracted by your feed; pull up your friends or followers list and work from there.

Be ruthless about unfollowing, unfriending, or muting people. You can always go check in on people later if you feel like it, but you have absolutely zero obligation to follow or friend anyone online, ever. There is tons of shit on the Internet, and you only want what feels good to be allowed into your world. It doesn't matter if someone intends to make you feel bad, or if you suspect that it's "your issues" that make you feel bad when you see their posts, just root out the bad feelings.

If you're worried that someone will get mad if you don't connect with them online, consider if that might be reason enough not to let them into your digital world. I know someone who will only friend a person online if one of them has been to the other's house. She wants her space to be as intimate as possible.

If that idea sounds cool to you, go for it! Or set your own standards for whom you follow. The most important thing is: only allow online connections from people who raise your personal vibration.

Do a yoga deep dive!

As I mentioned before, yoga isn't just for bendy, skinny people who call themselves yogis; it is a thousands-of-years-old practice that is free and available to all of us at any time.

What makes yoga so great is that it's a mind-body practice. It can offer your body anything from a lovely light stretch to a bitchin' workout (your choice), and at the same time, it can help to calm your mind and ground you into your own body and breath.

You can do yoga for, like, two minutes by looking up a pose online—or you can go to a yoga class and do sixty to ninety minutes with a teacher. I also love something in between: online classes with Yoga by Adriene. She has thousands of free classes on YouTube and even more with a paid subscription. Or there are a ton of other online (and offline!) yoga teachers; find one you resonate with.

Online or in person—whatever appeals to you—give it a go. Yoga has broad appeal for a reason. *Namaste* breathing!

Helpful Tip

If a teacher ever says or does something that makes you feel bad about yourself, move on to a different one. I promise: there is nothing wrong with your body, or your practice. Your injuries and modifications are beautiful. Your slow days are as important as your fast ones. Yoga is about you connecting to you, so follow your instincts, always.

Hour-ish
Practices

There is a saying in the meditation world: meditate for twenty minutes every day, but if you don't have twenty minutes to spare, do it for an hour. Ha!

When we find ourselves in these times of our lives where we feel like we can barely carve out two seconds to breathe, often what helps us the most is setting aside everything "urgent" and giving ourselves some serious "me time." Sometimes we are so caught up in the spiral of life that we have to get super serious about putting ourselves first. Think of the oxygen mask metaphor: you've got to take care of your own basic needs before you can help others with theirs.

I know you know this already, but I also know that it's easy to say you'll do it later—but stress really adds up over time, friends. You deserve to be healthy. So, let's do this!

TIME: 1 HOUR-ISH

Closet fitting

Get rid of everything in your closet that doesn't fit you well right now. Only keep things in your closet and drawers that both fit your body *and* make you feel good when you wear them. (A shirt that's too short in the belly or has us covering up the pilling underarms all day is not one that makes us feel good, no matter how awesome it was to begin with.)

When we clean our closets in this way, we will be able to more easily see what we have, get rid of psychic baggage along with the mess, and make room for new possibilities.

For many years, my daughter and I have done twice-yearly closet purges where the rule is, "If you don't love it, it's a no." You can like something a lot, but if you don't love it, it's a no. Marie Kondo, of course, has her own awesome rule: it has to spark joy. Her book and TV show can be super inspirational when it's time to let things go.

Once more for those in the back: get rid of everything that doesn't fit you right now, today. And if you don't absolutely love it, it's a no.

 ### *Helpful Tip*

If you must keep things for sentimental reasons, or because you think you are going to gain/lose weight, store them far away and out of sight. But hear this: "goal clothes" are a crappy, continual reminder that you aren't happy with yourself as you are; get rid of any of them immediately. If you get to your goal weight later, it will be fun to get some new duds. If you don't ever get there, you won't have a constant reminder of it. Let them go, seriously.

Take a photo walk

Photo walks are exactly what they sound like: you go on a meandering walk, and you take photos of what you come across.

You can do this solo, with friends, or I even once led a big group of strangers on a photo walk in Las Vegas for a conference I was speaking at. You can use a fancy camera if you have one, but your phone's camera is more than enough. (If you're using your phone, put it into Do Not Disturb or Airplane mode so you are not distracted.)

Walk, without aim or intention. Just notice what's around you and take pictures of what you are drawn to. It's fun to go on photo walks in new places, but it's just as interesting to do them close to home—it's like seeing the world in a whole new way. You can share the photos, or not. The point is to notice things while exercising a little creativity.

Helpful Tip

If you post your photos to Instagram, tag them with #effthisphotowalk—or browse the hashtag to see what others have discovered on their walks!

Forest bathing

First embraced in Japanese culture in the 1980s, forest bathing has swept the world. At its core, forest bathing is about spending concentrated time among the trees, soaking up the nature and connecting with the Earth. Don't worry about the name of this practice—we're really just going out into nature and soaking it up in a concentrated way. Look for a place with as many trees as possible; parks, hiking trails, and forests are all great places.

Find as quiet a spot in nature as possible, and locate or create a comfortable place to sit. Spend a few minutes simply breathing deeply and feeling what it is like to be where you are. As you start to unwind, begin to slowly pay attention to the following things:

- ☐ What sounds do you hear?
- ☐ What smells are making their way into your awareness?
- ☐ Notice the way the air feels: the temperature, the texture, the movement.
- ☐ Look around. What do you see? What is moving? What is staying still? What colors and shapes do you see? What is the quality of the light?
- ☐ Touch something. How does it feel? Is it squishy, scratchy, crumbly, or something else?
- ☐ At the beginning and again at the end of the practice, ask yourself: how does your body feel?
- ☐ What is your breathing like? What is your mind doing?

Spend a few minutes, at least, noticing each individual sense. Try to spend the whole hour just soaking it in (although any amount of time will benefit you). This practice is not about movement; it's about stillness and awareness. Let those qualities in. If you want to move, feel free to wander aimlessly but slowly, touching the trees and other things around you, and continually checking in with your senses. This isn't about exercise, but about connecting deeply to the natural world we live in.

Relax, and enjoy Mother Nature!

Helpful Tip

Ideally, you won't have your phone with you, but if that's truly not an option, put it on Do Not Disturb or Airplane mode so you can really focus on being still and aware.

Create a beautiful meal

What makes something special? A decision to treat it as special!

So, make your next meal into something beautiful: set a gorgeous table, play some chill music, maybe even light some candles or grab some flowers. Cook something from the heart (or simply serve take-out on your fanciest plates).

The first sense we engage when eating is often our eyes; creating a beautiful meal can start to sate us just by looking at it. A beautiful-looking plate of food can actually make us salivate—the first step in healthy digestion! And a colorful dish is often one that is full of the biggest variety of foods, particularly fruits and vegetables.

You can create a gorgeous meal even if you're dining solo (I've enjoyed this a great deal) or are eating with the usual suspects. Your choice to make it special is what creates the magic.

Helpful Tips

If you don't have time to cook a beautiful meal, you can still make it gorgeous. I've served guests take-out on my best place settings before, complete with linen napkins and freshly cut flowers.

To enjoy it even more, set a "no screens" rule for the meal. For a large group, I sometimes collect phones in a beautiful box and give them back after dessert. People may roll their eyes at first, but most are secretly (or eventually) relieved.

Watch a nature documentary

Oh my gosh, you guys, nature documentaries have gotten SO GOOD! I remember such boring movies in elementary school; someone always fell asleep at their desk (sometimes it was me). It's not like that anymore; they have become highly immersive, cinematic experiences.

And here's something cool: even though you're at home, when you look at scenes of nature, you still get some of the benefits of actually being outside, such as reduced stress. Watching nature documentaries can also help you become more aware of your own environment, inspire you to visit or learn more about new places, and stay in closer touch with our universal mother, Mama Earth.

Visit a museum

It's a myth of museums that you have to spend an entire day at them—a myth that I myself bought into for too many years. Visit a small museum, or a big one, for just a short time—you can always go back if you want to!

Or check out your local historical society, or, heck, even a flea market. We're just exploring and soaking up the inspiration.

Helpful Tips

If you can't get to a museum, explore one online! My friend Wendy Woon, who is the director of education at the Museum of Modern Art (MoMA), recommends checking out Google's Art Project. As she told me, "It has brought together works from collections in museums all over the world. This is the best aggregated resource." So go explore!

Stuck inside? Search for "The Agoraphobic Traveller" online to see a beautiful way that one anxiety-prone woman creates art as she explores the world from home.

Play with a kid

If you enjoy spending time with them, playing with children—your own or those of close friends—can be a great way to focus on what matters most: human connection. In this era of near-constant screen time, to give a child your undivided attention is a true gift. And, bonus: you get the gift, too.

If you're "borrowing" a friend's child for this, make sure, of course, that you've got permission from the parents first—but many parents are all too happy to have some help! Stuck on what to do? Try drawing your dream houses and then presenting them to each other, or going on a nature collection walk (see #084).

Helpful Tips

If you don't like kids, play with a pet instead! I have a friend who loves dogs but can't have one, so he carries dog treats in his pockets when he takes walks. It's very effective! (Be sure to ask permission first, of course.)

If you are a parent who feels decidedly unrelaxed by the idea of spending even more time with your little ones, consider dedicating a block of time to do whatever your little one(s) want to do. Some quality time can be incredibly bonding and relaxing for all! And if this seems like too much, ask a trusted a loved one or close friend to play with your kiddo(s) instead and give yourself a break.

Take a nature walk

Take a walk with the sole purpose of checking out what nature has to show you today.

My sister Cori often takes her son, Grey, on nature walks around and outside of Portland, Oregon, where they live. They hike and camp, sometimes for days at a time. I'm always amazed to see what they find: ferns, waterfalls, and so many mushrooms!

You don't have to save this one for when you are "in" nature, though. I live in New York City and I can do this there. Observe the nature around you, wherever you are.

I enjoy collecting nature on these walks; my house is brimming with shells, sponges, sand, branches, leaves, rocks, and all manner of treasures. If this sounds fun, try it! (Just make sure not to take anything that nature needs.)

Or make it a "trash walk"; bring a bag to collect the trash you come across as you go. There, you made the world a slightly better place! I do a lot of these and find them very meditative.

Try an unfamiliar healing modality

Different cultures have used a variety of healing techniques for thousands of years. Although some may be unfamiliar, many people experience great benefits from incorporating healing therapies into their lives.

Healing modalities can be a great complement to Western medicine—which is good at some things and bad at others. They can reduce stress, encourage self-healing, and move you towards mind-body wellness.

There is an endless variety of healing modalities, and different ones work best for different bodies. Many people have had massages, and at least heard of acupuncture, but there are so many more to explore and try. Some that have worked well for me throughout the years are Craniosacral therapy, Alexander technique (posture work), reiki (energy healing), cupping, gua sha, and breathwork. Other people like Bach flower remedies, Rolfing, Chinese herbal therapy, Ayurveda, biofeedback, chakra balancing, Mayan abdominal massage, and Emotional Freedom Technique (EFT—also known as tapping).

Follow your instincts about what to try. If energy healing feels too "out there" for you, consider acupuncture or a massage instead. Open your mind a little to the possibilities and trust your gut about what to try. If one doesn't jive, that's cool; try another. There are great benefits to be had in exploring what's out there—and if you try nothing more exotic than a massage, you'll still come out ahead.

Volunteer

Volunteering is one of those things that we all mean to do, and so rarely actually do. It can be hard to get started, awkward to go somewhere where you don't know anyone, and difficult to "find" the time. But volunteer work can be kind of magical: we go into it ready to help someone else, but we often end up being the ones who benefit the most.

Museums, libraries, food pantries, shelters of all kinds, refugee resettlement groups, parks . . . there are so many organizations doing good in the world that can use your help. Personally, I have loved my time spent building housing with Habitat for Humanity, and volunteering with homeless LGBTQIA youth.

Find a place where you can commit an hour of your time.

Not sure where to start? Think about what you're passionate about—maybe social justice, or animal welfare? Or go online and search volunteer opportunities in your area for ideas to get you started. Don't let good intentions stop you from doing the right thing! Just go for it.

Helpful Tip

Avoid spending your time with any group that has an attitude of swooping in and "saving" other humans; focus instead on the many organizations that empower and are an integral part of the communities they serve. Be open to going beyond "name brand" non-profits and working with grassroots and community-based groups.

Try outdoor exercise

Exercising outside gives you a double bonus: the mood-boosting benefits of exercise combined with the stress-busting side effects of being outside. Win-win!

Many of us work out in gyms or indoor fitness classes, if at all, and so taking a workout out of doors can be a brilliant way to both shake up our fitness routine (or get us moving), and to expose us to the fresh air that we could all use more of. Another nice bonus is that a lot of times when we exercise outside, it feels more like fun than the usual gym workout.

There are so many options for outdoor exercise: riding a bike, outdoor yoga, volleyball, tennis, kayaking, rock climbing, skiing or snowboarding, stand-up paddleboarding, running along the water, basketball, softball, handball, snorkeling, open-water swimming, snowshoeing . . . the list is endless. The point is just to get out and go. Don't let a lack of equipment or experience deter you, though— this can be as simple as a brisk walk in a local park.

If you try something and don't take to it, that's totally cool; just try a different thing next time. And who knows, you might fall in love with a new outdoor routine. Just get outside, and relax into the way it feels to be surrounded by fresh air and nature while you move your body.

Helpful Tip

 This is a great activity to do with someone else or in a group.

Connect with your inner activist

You don't need to be reminded that we are living in unprecedented times. Environmental catastrophe is nearing the point of no return, income inequality is at an unsustainably high rate, hate crimes are on the rise, and the civil rights of already marginalized people are, frankly, being trampled.

It can be terrifying, and for the sake of our own sanity, sometimes we have to focus on our own small worlds. But not always—we can move forward with our own lives while still taking time out to fight for what's right. In fact, I would argue that if you're lucky enough to be able to tune out this stuff sometimes, you're in the vital position of needing to stand up and speak out for people who are living in the trenches every day.

So, spend an hour engaging your inner activist, whatever that might look like.

In an hour, you can call your representatives to demand that they represent your values, attend a rally, or write postcards to voters. You can donate time or money (or both!) to causes that you believe in or educate yourself about disinformation campaigns and conspiracy theories so that you can better understand how they spread. You can educate yourself about civil discourse or attend a class about how to be a better ally.

Although it's super easy to want to disengage in times like these, it's imperative that we remain active.

Go on a dessert walk

It can be really fun to combine physical activity with a delicious treat. Depending on your own preferences and physical abilities, try one of the following:

- ☐ Dessert walk: walk a mile to an ice cream place. Have a scoop. Walk another mile to a pie place. Split a piece.
- ☐ Beer run: go for a half-hour run to a bar a couple of miles away. Enjoy a beer. Call a car home.
- ☐ Bike and baked goods: bike a few miles to a bakery. Have a treat and a cold drink. Grab another treat for when you get home.

Any combination that sounds fun to you is the right one to try; don't be limited to what I've suggested here. What we're going for is a little physical exertion, rewarded with a treat.

I know a couple who spent one very long day walking to all eleven ice cream shops in their hometown. I can't imagine having the endurance to eat all of that ice cream but I love the story that they get to tell—and now they know who has the best frozen treats in town!

Longer Practices

The little things can make a big difference . . . and the big things can lead to massive change.

While we might constantly say, "I need a vacation!" the truth is that society as a whole is taking less and less time off of work. Yes, take vacations! But don't wait until vacation time to take some quality time out of the day-to-day routine to connect with family, friends, and, most importantly, yourself. Relax, connect, and seek out some inspiration. Nothing could be more important.

Take a digital detox day

Spend a full day detoxing from all screen-based technology.

No email, no social media, no games on your phone, no TV or movies, no news. Many people find this incredibly difficult at first, but it's a great way to gently remind your brain that we don't need to be constantly connected. Our phones are designed to be addictive, and occasionally logging off helps us to break the cycle of the endless scroll/swipe/refresh.

If you need to, let people know what's happening ahead of time and give them an alternative way to contact you, or agree to check for missed calls at a certain time.

Spend the day noticing how it feels. Is it scary, weird, or a relief? How do you feel when the day is coming to a close? Have you noticed any changes? When do you crave screens the most? No judgment, we're just noticing how it feels. Reminding ourselves of the option and our ability to disconnect is great for our mental health.

Helpful Tip

Disconnect for a week, or a month, or do it once a month, every month. For myself, twice a year (typically January and August), I like to take a month-long break from social media and news. It's always hard at first, but when I re-engage after the month, I'm always surprised at how little I missed.

Take a day trip

Where? Anywhere!

Is there a museum, a cute town, or a roadside attraction you've always said you would check out someday? Today is that day! Load up your car (or book a ticket on a train or bus) and spend the day away. It doesn't matter where you go, as long as it sounds enjoyable to you.

This is a full day off of work and other responsibilities (choose to do this on a workday, or during the a weekend, or whatever fits into your schedule best). Do what you have to do to block the time off: delete apps from your phone, set your email autoresponder, and tell people you'll be away.

Helpful Tip

Not sure where to go? Just . . . go! Set out with the intention of staying out the whole day. Meander aimlessly and see where you end up.

Host a game night

People love to groan about playing organized games, but more than that, they love to play them.

Invite a friend (or five) over, and have a no-phones, no-pressure, silly-fun game night. Set out snacks, put on some great background music, rearrange the furniture, and if you feel like it, come up with some cheesy prizes.

You might want to have a few options so that when fatigue sets in on one game, you can move to the next. It's a good idea to offer different types of games so that a variety of people can do well.

Keep it light-hearted; this is about hanging out, not winning out. If you're worried about any of your guests being overly competitive, you can choose to play cooperative board games, where everyone is working toward the same goal (my family likes Forbidden Island for this; search online for more). Subjectively judged games like Apples to Apples can also be great for this.

✳ *Helpful Tip*

Game nights can be done for next to no cost. Ask everyone to contribute to the food and drinks, play charades or a drawing game based on clues you find online, and dig up goofy prizes from your stash of things you've been meaning to donate.

Spa day!

If you have the resources, book yourself a luxurious spa day. Have a couple of treatments and give yourself plenty of time to take advantage of the relaxing environment.

Or you can create just as beautiful and relaxing a situation for yourself at home with a little bit of planning and creativity.

Take stock of what you already have at home and re-create the parts of the spa experience that appeal to you most. Start by choosing from these (or do them all!):

- ☐ Relaxing music.
- ☐ Candles and dim lighting.
- ☐ Water with cucumber (or mint, or fruit) or herbal tea.
- ☐ Self-massage (try a foot or hand rub).
- ☐ A salt bath (see #072).

- ☐ Body scrub.
- ☐ Face masks.
- ☐ Hair treatments.
- ☐ Relaxing reading materials.
- ☐ Foot soak and scrub.
- ☐ Your most comfy towels, robe, slippers, and PJs.

Helpful Tip

I love doing an indulgent at-home spa day by myself; I find it super relaxing, and I love the solitude. But it's also a very fun thing to do with someone else. And when you have a friend participating, the prep work and cleanup time are halved!

Buy a plant

Plants, yes! They clean the air in our homes and offices, give us a little way to connect with Mama Earth, and are pleasant to look at. Buy a plant and give it regular love.

I try to spoil my plants; I mist them once a week and tell them that I am glad they are alive. I play them classical music sometimes. It's amazing what a little music can do for all living things.

See a live performance

The energy exchange of a live performance can be remarkable.

Choose whatever appeals the most to you: a play or musical, an arena rock show or an intimate live music venue, modern or classical dance, comedy, a lecture, a live podcast, avant-garde theater, a karaoke bar . . . what it is isn't the important part, only that it sounds fun to you. What matters the most here is that you are getting out and supporting other people who are putting their energy out into the world, and you will get to soak up the shared performance.

Take an art class

Remember: we're trying to balance consumption with creation. We're not necessarily trying to launch a new career (or even start a new hobby), but we do want to make things simply for the sake of making them.

Years ago, I took a painting class. We were asked to mix black and white paint together to create a grayscale with ten steps in it. I was terrible at it. Me, the person who keeps both her closet and her bookshelves permanently arranged by color gradient. It made me appreciate painters on a whole new level.

Sign up for an art class (in person if you can, or online if that's the route in) and just . . . enjoy the process. See what you learn. See what you love, and hate, and are inspired by and drawn to.

Maybe you'll be amazing at it, but probably you won't be. Not the point! Just create.

 Helpful Tip

If you can't devote the time to a class, choose to gather some materials from home and make some art instead. A collage, a diorama, a drawing, a craft stick model of the Empire State Building . . . whatever strikes your fancy. Maybe share it, maybe don't. Just create a little something with your hands.

Watch a feel-good movie

Watch a classic, feel-good movie.

Movie choices are very personal, so select one that makes you feel happy when you watch it. Start a list of your own feel-good movies, and add to it as you think of them.

You can even have a full-on immersive movie night! Rearrange the furniture, make popcorn, and enforce a no-phones rule. In this world of constant distractions, having an excuse to only focus on one thing can bring sweet relief. This is fun for both kids and adults.

Helpful Tip

CAN'T THINK OF ONE? SOME MOVIES TO CONSIDER:

Last Holiday	*Moana*	*Clueless*
The Birdcage	*The Princess Bride*	*Inside Out*

Take a hike

If getting outside for a moment, or even just looking at pictures of nature, can start to relieve stress, think about what spending a few hours (or even longer) outside can do for your body and mind.

It's time to really get out there—it's time to take a hike! This doesn't have to be a super-challenging hike, the point is to relax in nature, so there is no need to push yourself way beyond your comfort limit. Many state or national parks have lovely trails for beginners, and the internet is rife with information about a huge variety of hikes in virtually all inhabited places on Earth.

Don't use mildly bad weather as an excuse to stay inside—if the weather is subpar, prepare for it. Sunscreen and hats, or heat packs worn under layers, or extra socks and a raincoat . . . whatever you need to do to look after your own comfort, do it. If the weather is dangerous, do something inside. But otherwise, get on out! Nature has a lot of surprises waiting for you.

However you do this: enjoy the view, breathe in the fresh air, and enjoy disconnecting from the hustle of everyday life and reconnecting to the planet that supports us.

Helpful Tip

Consider meditating or doing a breathing exercise out in nature. Soak it in!

If your mobility is limited, adjust this practice to your own capabilities. Use a mobility aid, research trails that are appropriate for you, or turn the hike into a picnic instead. However you can comfortably do this is the perfect way for you.

Set Yourself up
for Success

Anyone who's ever worked for me has had the chance to grow sick of me asking, "What are you doing to set yourself up for future success?" Which is to say: I believe strongly in giving gifts to our future selves: the gifts of clarity, of health, of being prepared for things to go wrong.

In fact, I used to think of myself as a "worrier," but as I've grown, I've begun to think of anticipating problems as one of my superpowers! Preparing for the possibility of things going wrong, for me, actually helps me worry less.

And it's not just about anticipating problems: setting ourselves up for success can mean something as simple as putting together a playlist to listen to when we feel down, or as important as writing our own personal mission statement to refer back to when we could use a reminder about who we are, where we want to go, and how we want to get there.

It can be especially challenging to mute the never-ending daily fire alarms and focus on our futures, but nothing could be more important. Do some of these. You'll thank yourself!

Create a pick-me-up playlist

Take the time to make a music playlist that really revs your engine—or cools it down! Music can transport us, blast open our hearts, and put us into a completely different frame of mind. Make a personalized playlist (or several!) that you can come back to again and again.

It will need care and feeding, and that's okay: keep adding to it, delete songs when you are "over" them. I also like to have playlists that are instrumental only; sometimes I don't want to get engaged in someone else's story. Whatever is music to your ears is the perfect thing to put on your personalized pick-me-up playlist.

#rockon

Blue light makeover

Blue light is simply the short-wavelength, high-energy part of the visible light spectrum. Natural sunlight is the main source of blue light, and things were all good when the rhythm of our days was matched to the sun. But when we started staring at screens for hours and hours after the sun went down, and using LED lights in our homes, we really started messing with our own circadian rhythms.

Blue light is what causes digital eyestrain (it also flickers a lot), it makes it harder for us to get to sleep, and it is thought to damage our skin due to premature aging. (We use sunblock when we go outside but then sit inches from our screens all day. Whoops!)

It is, frankly, a scourge of modern life that is affecting us in many ways that we are not even aware of. So let's do something about it! Your blue light makeover is about drastically reducing the amount of blue light you are exposed to when the sun is down.

If you have an iPhone, turn on Apple's Night Shift mode (or research how to set up a similar feature on your own phone). Research and download an app on your computer to have it automatically adjust to the changing natural light. Swap out any LED or fluorescent bulbs in your home for warmer bulbs. Stop all screen exposure a full hour before bedtime (yes, including your phone). Wear blue blocking glasses at home at night.

Pay close attention to all of the ways in which you are exposed to blue light after sunset, and take the necessary steps to eliminate or drastically reduce them. Your eyes—and your sleep—will thank you!

Real meals

It's fine: not all meals can be beautiful, nutritionally packed gardens of delight and deliciousness. But some can be!

Make a commitment that your next meal will be packed full of whatever nutrients your body is telling you it needs right now. Listen past the cravings for quick sugar/carb energy and lean into whatever your body needs. It might be cooked greens, healthy fats, or lean protein. Your body is actually pretty smart at asking for what it needs if you take the time to listen to it. Tune in, learn, and give your body what it wants.

Be sure to also take the time to enjoy the meal—and pay attention to how it makes you feel! Listening to what your body wants—and to when it has had enough—are essential parts of more mindful eating.

Once I ate an entire watermelon for dinner, felt terrible about it, confessed to my nutritionist, and she congratulated me for listening to what my body wanted. Ha! (I hope it goes without saying that I am not recommending that you eat an entire watermelon for dinner. But hey, sometimes the body wants a what it wants.)

Love that body

We all have great intentions when it comes to taking care of our bodies. But the path to hell, my Grandma Iris once told me, is paved with good intentions. (She had tons of great wisdom.)

Now is the time to do that one healthy body thing you've been putting off. This is not about improvement—this is about taking care of your beautiful body and mind. Maybe you can finally make an appointment for a skin check or way-overdue annual physical, get an eye exam, visit a new gym, attend that meditation class, etc.

You only have to do one thing. But do it today.

Helpful Tips

If you don't have good medical insurance because you live in the US and the health care system is a scary mess, or for any other reason, I am so sorry. It's complete and total BS. But! You can still take care of yourself, and, in fact, there's all the more reason to. Maybe you finally get on a waiting list at the free clinic, make an appointment with Planned Parenthood, or load up on free meditation apps. As much as you are able to, don't let lack of money (or insurance) get in the way of your fabulous self-care.

If you, like me, suffer from chronic or serious illness, sometimes thinking even more about taking care of your health is the last thing you want to do. If that's the case, I suggest doing exercise #065 instead.

#103

TIME: 1 HOUR OR LONGER

Sleep makeover

Oh, baby . . . you deserve to get good sleep. It makes all of the difference in the world. Ideally, we sleep for roughly a third of our lives. If you live to the age of seventy-five, that puts you at twenty-five years in bed. But about half of us are sleep deprived. It's not just a matter of being tired; sleep deprivation can cause all sorts of serious problems, ranging from decline in cognitive ability (it makes us dumber) to a higher risk of a lot of health issues (from stroke to heart disease), higher rates of depression and weight gain, and weakened immunity.

Let's make those years in bed count!

Obviously, we want to allow for more time to sleep, so do as much as you can to make the time. But there are plenty of other things you can do to improve the *quality* of your sleep as well. Take your pick from what makes sense:

- Remove all clutter from the bedroom.
- Ban all screens from the bedroom (and none anywhere an hour before bedtime).
- Use a real alarm clock (instead of your phone—charge that in another room).
- Consider white-noise machines.
- Install blackout and/or sound-dampening curtains.
- Use humidifiers or fans.
- Invest in a super comfortable mattress.
- Buy bed linens that feel great.
- Make or buy a linen spray with real lavender or other sleep-inducing scents.

- Consider natural sleep supplements, such as melatonin.
- Try sleep-inducing beverages, such as golden milk or chamomile tea.
- Try a bath before bedtime (a great time to read a book for pleasure).
- Stick to a routine that works for you.

Choose any or all of the above or do some research into other things that work for people.

Discipline in sleep pays off in big ways across the rest of your life.

Helpful Tip

If you find yourself lying awake at night, the book *Goodnight Mind* by Colleen E. Carney and Rachel Manber is a great primer about why—and ways to cope.

Level up your commute

For a lot of people, the commute can reliably be the worst part of your day. While you might not be able to eliminate your commute, you can take steps to make it much less horrific, and possibly even pleasant.

It's commute makeover time! Consider:

SCENTS

If you commute in a car, invest in an essential oil diffuser and play around with which scents are best for the beginning and end of the day. If you take public transit, bring along a little rollerball of scent.

SOUNDS

Download podcasts and music to your phone so that you are always prepared. You don't want to get stuck with crappy radio commercials or the conversations of other stressed-out people. I try to always have several podcasts fully downloaded as well as multiple playlists synced to my phone. I have good headphones, so I can listen without bothering other people with my noise choices. Bring an extra charger if you might need one. Creating your own scent and sound bubble will go a long way.

COMFORT

Even my friends who work at fancy NYC-based luxury fashion brands change into more practical shoes for their commutes. Don't hobble yourself, my high-heel-loving friends. Plan ahead to be warm, safe, and comfy. I almost always have a cashmere scarf with me (silk-blend for summer, and thick-as-a-blanket for winter), because I get cold super easily. Bring an umbrella if you might need one. I also keep a black tourmaline and a rose quartz crystal in my bag, because I read that they are good for protection during travel, and I love holding them. What makes you feel good?

METHOD

If you use a car on your daily commute, you are a lucky sun-on-a-beach because you can create a little world of your own making! (Those of us who take public transit have to carry our commutes with us.) If you are going to be stuck in traffic, do it in your rose-scented, succulent-growing, beats-blasting machine, swaddled in a blanket, eating a snack, and in your house slippers with fresh air running through your hair.

Speaking of fresh air, is there a way to get more of it? Can you bike? Take a boat? Walk part of the way? Really try to find a way to incorporate some Mother Nature into your day.

TIME

What can you do to regularly give yourself more time for your commute? Rushing sucks.

Helpful Tips

Work from home? Try upgrading your work space and your routine instead. Same categories apply.

As you commute, you may come across people who are less fortunate than you. I always keep a handful of bills paper-clipped to a "You Are Beautiful" sticker. I consider carrying these to be part of my commute routine.

Tweak your morning

It's a big personal push of mine to always be trying to set up my future self for success. (In my house, we like to say, "I'm giving a gift to my future self!") One of the best ways to do that, I've found, is to pay very close attention to routines. Our morning routines might be the most important ones: mornings set the stage for the entire day, and the tone we create will ultimately carry through.

Spend some time thinking about your own mornings: what works well for you? What seems to cause stress over and over again? What can you do the night before to make mornings run more smoothly? Once you have a clear idea of where the rough edges are, you can start to try out different tactics for reducing the friction.

Some options to get you started:

- Create the time to spend a few dedicated moments reviewing the day ahead.
- Select your entire outfit the night before (undergarments, shoes, everything).
- Pack bags completely the night before.
- Prepare breakfast options on Sunday and freeze half (think: frittatas, granola, pancakes, or smoothie mixes).
- Try reading for pleasure in the mornings—set a timer and dive into your book.
- Exercise in the mornings (even if it's just a few simple yoga stretches).

- Set an intention for the day, such as "I will be fully present," or "I will practice forgiveness," or even "I will keep my eye on the prize." **(See #013 for more about intention setting.)**

- Experiment with a morning meditation practice (solo, with an app, or a guided video).

- Journal **(see #059).**

- Do a little morning drink detox; try having warm lemon water before coffee.

- When you get to work, commit to tackling your highest priority thing first.

- Leave for your commute earlier than usual. **(See #039 and #074.)**

Helpful Tip

Need inspiration? Search the Web; there are endless articles about morning routines, ranging from the overscheduled to the truly bizarre. Morning routines vary wildly from person to person, but they really matter for each of us.

"From the desk of . . . you!"

It is so much easier (and you're more likely!) to send a quick note of thanks/congratulations, etc. if you have all of the supplies at hand. So, spend some time gathering thank-you notes, postcards, blank notes, beautiful pens, and—very important—lots of stamps!

Stock up on fun things to put in notes. Designate a drawer or a box where all of these things live so that you can find it all in a hurry. An up-to-date address book makes this a lot easier, too, so get yours into shape.

We have a drawer of cards in our house that's organized by category: thank-you cards, birthday cards, belated birthday cards, congratulatory messages, condolences, etc. We never hesitate to buy cool cards when we see them, because we know they will get used someday. You can spend a lot on stationery (personalized engraving!), or very little (thrift stores often have boxes and boxes of cards). Whatever works best for you is perfect; the point is to set up your future self for success in staying in touch with the people you value in your life.

Helpful Tip

Set aside a regular day to send written notes. I try to do it on Sunday afternoons; because I already have the supplies, it only takes ten minutes or so—and it feels great.

Do a full-fledged
#MINDFULTECH
makeover

The technology that we use every day is intentionally designed to be addictive. It's not our fault, but it is our responsibility. If you find yourself staring at screens more than you'd like, don't beat yourself up—but do something about it.

To do a full-on Mindful Technology™ makeover, start by spending some dedicated time making your phone less addictive:

- ☐ Turn off all notifications that are not directly from a human being in real time. (Texts and phone calls are fine; news, email, or social media notifications are not—and mute all nonurgent group texts; you'll read them when you want to.)

- ☐ Delete all apps that you haven't used in the last couple of months.

- ☐ Put everything into folders; only have bare-bones apps on your home screen.

- ☐ Make it intentionally difficult to check your email or social media on your phone; save these things for your computer.

- ☐ Take all of your social media accounts off your phone. Delete all social media apps (including messaging apps), and log out of the site on your browser. This will save you time and help protect your personal data.

- ☐ Look at which apps have permission to use your microphone and remove as many as possible. Go to setting/microphone and delete where relevant. (Some apps will eavesdrop on you and sell data about your personal conversations!) Do the same thing for your location settings.

Write a personal mission statement

When we've answered the big questions—when we know our own core values, are in touch with our dreams, and are aware of what we prioritize the most in our lives—the smaller questions can answer themselves.

Having a personal mission statement, written by you and based on the most important priorities to you, can be a beautiful gift to yourself. It can help you to make decisions more easily, say no more often, and to have more confidence in your path.

With a personal mission statement, you can take what can feel like tough questions and potentially find simplified answers. You can keep yourself on track, and even inspire others to make more illuminated choices.

Set aside a few dedicated hours (or better yet, spread it out over a few days) to research other people's personal mission statements, ruminate on your value system, and write your own.

Helpful Tip

Sharing your mission statement can help you integrate it more fully into your daily life; consider posting it publicly or sharing it with the people who matter most to you.

LET'S STAY IN TOUCH!

I am generally super slow to respond (hey, I'm busy being mindful!) but I love hearing from you, and I would especially love to hear about your experiences putting this book into practice.

The best ways to stay in touch are:

My newsletter //
lizakindred.com/subscribe

On Twitter //
@LizaK

On Instagram //
@EFFTHISmeditation
@MindfulTechnology
@Liza_K

You can also search **#effthisbook** on Twitter and Instagram to see how other people are working with the book. And of course, don't forget that there are tons of free resources waiting for you on my website. You will have access to bonus tips; free versions of body scans; suggestions for movies, documentaries, podcasts, and social media pages to check out; affordable blue light–blocking glasses; a Mindful Technology™ worksheet for a full mindful makeover; a free guide to writing a personal mission statement; and much more by visiting my site at **effthismeditation.com/bookextras.**
To find out whether I'm available to hire to speak at your event, please visit **lizakindred.com/speaking**.

Lastly, don't forget the most important thing: be gentle with yourself.

PLEASE REMEMBER

Nothing in this book is meant to imply in any way that there is something wrong with you, or that you need to be fixed. You don't. You are complete; you are whole; you are worthy of love exactly the way you are right now.

This book offers practices and techniques to help you get out from under the craziness of the world, either momentarily, or, if you employ these practices often, for increasingly longer periods of time.

———

Some of these will work for you better than others: bookmark those, memorize them, or make a note in your phone or a notebook. If something doesn't feel good to you, don't do it, and please don't beat yourself up if something doesn't click.

Keep using the practices that work, and challenge yourself to try some new ones every once in a while. And try to stretch out the time you devote to these techniques a bit if you can. As that saying about meditation goes:

> If you can meditate for twenty minutes a day, do that. If you can't find the time to do twenty minutes, do an hour.

This book is loaded with short, easily accessible practices, because sometimes we literally only have one minute. But it has many longer practices as well, which offer deeper, richer kinds of self-love. Try some of the longer ones. It will pay off.

BIG THANKS!

So many lovely people contributed ideas to the book, and I can't thank them enough for their thoughts and their permission to share.

Dr. Aimée Derbes

Aizada Adamou

Alyson Pearson

Andy Vitale

Cathleen O'Connell

Cheryl Mitchell

Christopher James Cole

Cindy Clark

Dawn Philips

Jenn Sabin

Jes Sauser

Katherine Hopkins Druckman

Katrina Kindred

Kristina Frantz

Leslie Berg

Lisa Rex

Martha Garvey

Mary Beth Weaver

Melissa Sulewski

Morgan McCormick

Nga Nguyen

Pamela Stewart

Pete Dunlap

Ryan Szrama

Sheila Kindred

Stefanie Toftey

Susan Hinkle Norris

Teri Wood TeBockhorst

Wendy Woon

Zhaia Wineinger

ACKNOWLEDGMENTS

My health and well-being are due in no small part to my personal team of healers, wellness practitioners, and other supporters. It is because of them that I am able to continue to create and work despite years of chronic illness. Specifically: to call Pamela Stewart a massage therapist is to vastly underestimate her ability to heal, support, and empower; there is a reason we call her "Magic Hands Pam" in our house.

There is an enormous community of people I have interacted with online (some I have met in person and many I have not), thousands of people who have seen me speak around the globe. To every single one of you: thank you for your support. Every kind word, every tweet and "fave" and "like" and cute emoji—I feel the support in all of it and have endless gratitude. The tiny bits of support add up to an incredibly meaningful amount.

My family, both immediate and extended, have been among the biggest fans of my career. Thank you to them! My mom wants you to know that she wishes she had this book when she was younger, and I want you to know that it was her creativity that inspired it. My dad is the closest thing I have ever met to a living bodhisattva.

To my nieces and nephews: Ava, Jonah, Audra, Aliya, Monroe, Eric, Sloane, Grey, Quinn, my "adopted" daughter Amelie, and my lovely goddaughter Keira—and the rest of the little ones who are finding their way: remember to work hard, have fun, and let your light shine. You are perfect just the way you are.

I am also blessed to have an extremely supportive family and group of friends. All of my love goes to Blanca Burgoa, Maggie Romine, Wendy Woon, Kristina Frantz, Kelly Hoey, Alyssa Loren, Pavan Bahl, Amber Hathaway, Melissa Gonzalez, Adreanna Limbach, Kim Fasting- Berg, Carlos Garza, Jenn Mondi, Sarah Niska, Amanda Gilbert, and so many other wonderful people who I get to call my friends. Lodro Rinzler has been a friend, mentor, and teacher for many years. He has helped me shape my own voice as a meditation teacher and shown me how to be a whiskey-loving, profanity-using aspiring bodhisattva. You should read all of his books.

Sometimes people are wrestling with their own demons and make choices that add challenge to our lives. James Walker taught me to call these people Zen Masters. To these people, my own Zen Masters: thank you to you, too. You've helped me grow, even when I really, really didn't want to.

Since this is the acknowledgments section, let me also acknowledge that I have benefited from white privilege. My sister Katrina sent me a meme recently; it said, "Maybe you manifested it; maybe it's white privilege!" (Credit to *rise up! good witch* for the meme.) This cheeky post got to the root of why I don't push an agenda of "Just align yourself with the universe and it will happen," because our society offers different levels of opportunity to different people. I have benefited from systemic and entrenched racism. When I benefit, others lose out. I take that seriously, and pledge to do what I can to make the world a more equal place for all, both through my work and through my interpersonal relationships. I am in no way perfect, and I certainly don't have any answers, but I will continue to acknowledge, try to learn, and try to do what is right for all.

To the person who is reading this hoping to see their name: no one belongs here more than you. I love you.

The book you are holding in your hands was made possible by the support of Keyla Pizarro-Hernández as editor, Ashley Eddy as copywriter, and Amy Fuller of Flint Inc. as a fantastic, patient, kind, creative, funny, dedicated creative collaborator. This book is extra A.F. because of her. Thank you to Rage Kindelsperger at Quarto for shepherding my book into the world!

Without the endless support and encouragement of my husband, Josh Clark, this book would not exist. He believes in me, and in what I have to share with the world, in a way so pure and unwavering that it sometimes baffles me.

Not only has he been at my side through health challenges that have made my own light dim at times, but he also graciously and continually uses his own platforms to spotlight my ideas and champion my work. The clarity, context, and kindness that I get when he shines his spotlight on me are invaluable.

My daughter, Veronika, is the reason for everything good that I try to do in the world. I learn from her every day; she is gracious, funny, incredibly smart, and a good and kind human being. She has raised me well. Monkey, I adore you. (The proverbial "kids these days" always get a bad rap, but I am telling you from firsthand experience that many of today's young people work hard, care deeply, and will quite likely save our asses.)

Finally, to you: thank you for reading this book. Thank you for being open to new ideas. It means the world to me—and it means that together, we can change the world.

May you—and all beings—be happy.